DISCOVERING GIRARD

MICHAEL KIRWAN SJ

A COWLEY PUBLICATIONS BOOK

Lanham, Chicago, New York, Toronto, and Plymouth, UK

To my father

A Cowley Publications Book
Published by Rowman & Littlefield Publishers, Inc.
A wholly owned subsidiary of
The Rowman & Littlefield Publishing Group, Inc.
4501 Forbes Boulevard, Suite 200, Lanham, Maryland 20706
http://www.rowmanlittlefield.com

Estover Road, Plymouth PL6 7PY, United Kingdom

Distributed by National Book Network

Published by Darton, Longman and Todd, London, UK, 2004
Copyright © Michael Kirwan

Library of Congress Cataloging-in-Publication Data:
Kirwan, Michael.
    Discovering Girard / Michael Kirwan.
        p. cm.
    Includes bibliographical references and index.
    ISBN: 978-1-56101-229-9
2. Violence. 3. Imitation. 4. Scapegoat. 5. Philosophy, French—20th
century. 6. Philosophy, Modern—20th century. I. Title.
    B2430.G494K57 2005
    203'.4—dc22   2005008866

Cover art: *Don Quixote*, 1955 (gouache on paper) by Picasso, Pablo
(1881–1973). Private Collection, Peter Willi; www.bridgeman.co.uk.
© 2005 Estate of Pablo Picasso / Artists Rights Society (ARS), New York.

Cover design: Jennifer Hopcroft

♾™ The paper used in this publication meets the minimum requirements
of American National Standard for Information Sciences—Permanence
of Paper for Printed Library Materials, ANSI/NISO Z39.48-1992.

Printed in the United States of America

CONTENTS

INTRODUCTION

Without publicising it, Sancho Panza succeeded, over the years, in diverting his demon (whom he later called Don Quixote) away from himself. This he did through reading many novels of chivalry and crime in the evening and night hours, so that this demon set out unstoppably to do the craziest things. However, because of the lack of a pre-ordained object (which should have been Sancho Panza himself), these harmed no one. A free man, Sancho Panza serenely followed Don Quixote on his ways, perhaps out of a certain sense of responsibility, and had of them a great and edifying entertainment until the end of his days.

(Franz Kafka, *The Truth about Sancho Panza*)

We have no choice but to go back and forth, from alpha to omega. And these constant movements, this coming and going, force us to construct matters in a convoluted, spiraling fashion, which eventually runs the risk of being unsettling and even incomprehensible for the reader . . . I think one needs to read [my work] like a thriller. All the elements are given at the beginning, but it is necessary to read to the very end for the meaning to become completely apparent.

(René Girard, *Celui par qui le scandale arrive*, pp. 87–8)

For over forty years the French American cultural critic, René Girard, has been writing a 'thriller' about culture, violence and the sacred. In a dozen books, and in numerous articles and interviews, he does indeed seem to shuffle obsessively back and forth, between a few key insights – like a detective or a spy-catcher, looking for the vital clues.

The question which possesses him is both ancient and still relevant: *what are we to make of religion?* This means asking about the origin and function of religion, and it also means getting to grips with a curious paradox. The paradox is this: in premodern societies, religion was accepted as the force which united a society and gave it cohesion (the Latin word is *religare*, 'to bind'), but in the modern era religion is largely treated with anxiety and suspicion, because it is seen as a source of division and conflict. For most people today, religion is safest when regarded as a matter of purely private concern. Professor Girard offers a way of understanding this paradox, though it is a theme which he feels can only be approached in an indirect way. To many who have tried to engage with his work, his admission that there is a necessary difficulty and obliqueness about his style will come as no surprise. Whether things are made any easier by reading Girard with the same gusto as we might read *Tinker Tailor Soldier Spy* or a classic Agatha Christie novel, is another question.

This intriguing comparison should not mislead us into seeing Girard's work as entertainment or literary escapism. Just the opposite is true: the urgency, the 'thrill' of Girard's work is the possibility of gaining original and challenging insights into some of our contemporary world's most agonising problems. Can we learn something about the complex interrelation between secular modernity and the religiously inspired terrorism which conceived the 11 September atrocity? Or about patterns of provocation and resistance, entrenched and ritualised in long-term conflicts such as Northern Ireland or the struggle for Palestine? Or about the bitter polemics concerning the 'sacredness' of life and reproductive 'rights' in the United States? Or about the kinds of stigma which attach to people living with HIV/AIDS? The excruciating questions about religion's ambiguous relation to different forms of violence are not new at all, but in the last four years have literally exploded into our awareness with a new ferocity. In fact, Girard's work has anticipated this very recent development by four decades – all the issues mentioned above have been addressed, either by Girard himself or by thinkers inspired by him, using the theoretical approach he has been developing.

In its literal sense, *theoria* means a 'looking at' evidence from a particular perspective. Or, to put this another way, a special kind of 'imagination', as this word is used by Archbishop Cauchon in the epilogue of George Bernard Shaw's *Saint Joan* (1924). Here is a conversation between two churchmen, one of whom, de Stogumber, is speaking of the traumatic effect upon him of witnessing St Joan's martyrdom:

DE STOGUMBER: Well, you see, I did a very cruel thing once because I did not know what cruelty was like. I had not seen it, you know. That is the great thing: you must see it. And then you are redeemed and saved.

CAUCHON: Were not the sufferings of our Lord Christ enough for you?

DE STOGUMBER: No. Oh no: not at all. I had seen them in pictures, and read of them in books, and been greatly moved by them, as I thought. But it was no use: it was not our Lord that redeemed me, but a young woman whom I saw actually burned to death. It was dreadful: oh, most dreadful. But it saved me. I have been a different man ever since, though a little astray in my wits sometimes.

CAUCHON: Must then a Christ perish in torment in every age to save those that have no imagination?

There is surely a touch of racism here: Cauchon is French, so he naturally feels superior to the less sophisticated, less 'imaginative' Englishman. And Cauchon does seem to be right, up to a point. When human beings behave cruelly and atrociously – 'man's inhumanity to man' – their actions suggest something like a catastrophic failure of imagination, a sheer incapacity to put themselves in the place of the victim who is being abused, tortured, or made to disappear. In the worst cases, such as genocide, there is even a refusal to acknowledge that the victims are human beings at all. As for de Stogumber, there is pathos in what he says about the inadequacy of even the holiest representation compared to 'the real thing', and about his capacity for deceiving himself, even about his own experience: 'I had been greatly moved – as I thought.'

Girard is concerned with some of the same issues explored in Shaw's play: the representation of martyrdom and suffering, the adequacy of the Christian revelation. But there is one important difference which we can point to straightaway. Shaw's character Cauchon rather superciliously implies that this 'imagination', the correct and humane way of looking at things, is somehow an obvious or natural point of view. Christ has shown us the meaning and reality of suffering, and that should be enough. Only the asinine dullness of (other) people stands in the way of our creating a truly sympathetic and harmonious world. Those like Cauchon (and of course Shaw!), who happen to be blessed with intelligence and sensitivity, can only roll their eyes in exasperation with the de Stogumbers of the world.

René Girard's tone is different, and more humble. His interest in this 'perspective of the victim' began as a close reading of important works of literature, from authors such as Proust, Dostoevsky and Shakespeare. Later he turned his attention to anthropological and mythical texts (especially the Oedipus and Dionysus cycles), and later still to close readings of the Jewish and Christian scriptures. These varied sources have convinced him that this power of empathetic imagining, far from being something that we should expect of human beings, much less take for granted, is actually something miraculous. If we look at the history of the world and its civilisations, imaginative sympathy for the victim is in fact a very rare quality. In most cultures, the exact opposite applies, because the weak and vanquished have no rights at all. If and when this sympathy comes about, it does so as the result of a titanic struggle within a person and within a society. The struggle is nothing less than what de Stogumber describes as a kind of 'conversion'. And it is not just for the dull and unimaginative; it is a conversion which even some of the most sensitive and creative spirits known to humanity have had to undergo.

In the spring of 1959, after 26 years as an agnostic, Girard's work on five European novelists (Cervantes, Flaubert, Stendhal, Proust and Dostoevsky) had led him back to an interest in Christianity. To varying degrees, the life and work of each of these authors displayed a similar pattern: each author underwent a 'conversion' experience, which liberated him to go on and write his most important works. At the same time, Girard was impressed by a common concern in these writers, namely their understanding of the nature of desire as 'mimetic' or imitated (a concept we will explore in more detail below). The more mature the works of each of these authors, the more explicit and developed is their understanding of the mimeticism of desire. But even this interesting discovery by Girard would have remained on a purely intellectual level, if a sudden health scare had not intervened and caused him to reassess his own beliefs. The questions were now real-life and not just 'literary'. Girard returned to the Catholic Church he had left behind in his childhood, and 'mimetic theory' was born.

Put very simply, this is a theory which seeks to elucidate the relationships – one might say the complicity – between religion, culture and violence. It has become standard to describe the theory as having three parts: the mimetic nature of desire; the scapegoat mechanism as the way in which societies regulate the violence generated by mimetic competition; and the importance of the Gospel revelation as the way in which this scapegoat mechanism is exposed and rendered ineffective.

It would not be too schematic to suggest that the three phases correspond to three academic disciplines or approaches with which Girard has been involved: literature; cultural anthropology; and theology or biblical study. At the risk of being even more schematic, one could match off each of the three phases with one key book by Girard, namely *Deceit, Desire and the Novel* (French original, 1961), *Violence and the Sacred* (1972), and *Things Hidden since the Foundation of the World* (1978). It is the second of these books that caught and staggered the imagination, with *Le Monde* declaring that 'the year 1972 should be marked with an asterisk in the annals of the humanities'. A philosopher, Paul Dumouchel, sums up:

> Beginning from literary criticism and ending up with a general theory of culture, through an explanation of the role of religion in primitive societies and a radical reinterpretation of Christianity, René Girard has completely modified the landscape of the social sciences. Ethnology, history of religion, philosophy, psychoanalysis, psychology and literary criticism are explicitly mobilized in this enterprise. Theology, economics and political sciences, history and sociology – in short, all the social sciences, and those that used to be called moral sciences – are influenced by it.
>
> (Dumouchel, 1988, p. 23)

The first part of this book (Chapters 1–3) will be based around these three structural elements of mimetic theory: that our desires are to a large degree imitated or derived through 'mimesis'; that societies have a tendency to channel the violence which arises as a result of mimetic interaction by means of a process of 'scapegoating', which underlies not just religious practices (such as sacrifice) but also secular institutions; and finally, that the revelation which occurs in the Jewish and Christian scriptures is the primary force responsible for showing us the truth about this hidden violence, and for enabling alternative ways of structuring human living. I intend to look at some more abstract methodological reflections, as well as some of the principal objections to the theory (Chapter 4); and lastly to consider how the theory might develop in the future (Chapter 5). Each of the three expository chapters begins with a *précis* of its content.

In the remainder of this Introduction, I would like to address some particular features which help us understand why mimetic theory is so energising for some people, and so easily and vigorously dismissed by others. I hope light can be shed here by establishing five pointers or characteristics which will orientate us in the delicate task of 'discovering Girard'.

Firstly, as we have seen, René Girard admits to a difficulty within his own work, which he appears to suggest is unavoidable. The insight that is to be won is inseparable from a particular kind of intellectual struggle which the reader has to undertake – precisely like reading a challenging and convoluted espionage novel. Anyone diving headlong into *Violence and the Sacred* or *Things Hidden* can soon find themselves disoriented and discouraged by the sheer fertility of ideas and references. This difficulty should not be overstressed, however. Michel Serres has remarked that Girard's ideas can be understood by an 11-year-old child, and one gets the impression that this simplicity and accessibility is more off-putting for some academics than the alleged convolution of Girard's thought. Unlike some other contemporary theorists, who view language with such a mistrust that they seem to be working against the very medium in which they communicate, Girard believes in the possibility of communicating his ideas lucidly, and attempts to do so with humour and style.

Secondly, and related to this first point, there needs to be a clear distinction between René Girard's work, and 'mimetic theory' as such. The theory now has a life of its own, as other scholars take on its central insights and re-fashion them, even if they disagree with Girard on significant points. Since the early 1990s a Colloquium has been in existence for literary scholars, theologians, psychologists, lawyers, etc. 'to explore, criticise, and develop the mimetic model of the relationship between violence and religion in the genesis and maintenance of culture', so it has become very much a collaborative and interdisciplinary effort. One example of this should be mentioned here: Girard has in several contexts expressed his indebtedness to the work of the Swiss Jesuit theologian, the late Raymund Schwager, who made a highly significant theological appropriation of Girard's anthropology. While the present book is above all an elucidation of the thought of Girard, it will also seek to be attentive to these important collaborative influences, including that of Schwager and his colleagues at the University of Innsbruck.

The third point is a stylistic one, which affects the way Girard's writings should be approached. Girard has been described as the 'hedgehog' thinker who 'sees one thing', as opposed to the fox who 'sees many things'. Sometimes his eagerness to give testimony to his insight has led to over-reaching generalisations, which have then to be retracted or qualified. A prime example would be the discussion of 'sacrifice', which at first he refused to acknowledge as a suitable term to be used in the context of Christianity. Discussion with Schwager brought about a change of opinion on this, as he has readily acknowledged on a number of occasions. This in itself is unproblematic, except that the 'retractions' often appear in sources which are less accessible than his major works. As is customary with French intellectuals, he will often develop or nuance his theory in interviews (the 1986 *Festschrift* for Girard lists 29 published interviews, and there have been many more since then). So, anyone reading *Things Hidden* for an account of what Girard believes about sacrifice would be seriously misled, because of his change of emphasis since this book appeared in 1978.

For this reason, I have proposed a threefold division of Girard's work:
- three 'classic' texts (*Deceit, Desire and the Novel*; *Violence and the Sacred*; *Things Hidden since the Foundation of the World*)
- Girard's other books, consisting mainly of literary or biblical 'readings' in which mimetic theory is put to work (such as the books on Job, Dostoevsky, Shakespeare)
- important but less accessible sources, such as interviews in journals, or in books not translated into English, where significant developments of Girard's thought are set out. As it is the literature

in this third category which will be least familiar to a general English reader, I try to make special reference to it.

Fourthly, and to schematise this presentation even further, it is important to see the three parts of the mimetic theory as a conversation with some of the 'big guns' of modern thought. Much of what Girard has written is dependent upon the insights of three authors: Hegel, and more crucially Sigmund Freud, and Friedrich Nietzsche. Girard's judgement on the last two of these authors is the same: they come very close to the truth about mimetic desire, but do not quite make it over the finishing line, and in fact mislead us all the more because they are so near yet so far. This is why Girard's thinking may well have a familiar feel to it: his account of mimetic desire has clear affinities with Hegel's desire for 'recognition' by the other ('desiring the desire of another') as this is set out in the *Phenomenology of Spirit*; his account of violence as the origin of culture (otherwise referred to as 'originary violence') bears a strong resemblance to Freud's description of the primeval murder in *Totem and Taboo*; and Girard's endorsement of the Christian revelation is very precisely an acceptance of Nietzsche's challenge, 'Dionysus versus the Crucified' – except that where Nietzsche opts for Dionysus, Girard chooses the Crucified. As a coda to each of the individual chapters – on mimetic desire, scapegoating, biblical revelation – I will offer a brief analysis of each of these three important philosophical themes, in so far as they have an impact on Girard's project.

A fifth and final point returns us to the literary theme with which we began. Girard is not afraid to think on the large scale: he offers a general theory of religion, and is prepared to take issue with major figures like Freud and Nietzsche. Much of the critical resistance to Girard stems from a judgement that this kind of thinking is outdated and inappropriate. This charge will be examined more closely in Chapter 4 below, but in any case it can be said that Girard's main interest, his passion, lies elsewhere. From his earliest training as decipherer of medieval manuscripts, Girard has always been, quite simply, a reader of texts. He enjoys writing and talking about the great novelists and playwrights (at least those whose writings promise fertile ground for his theory), and seems in the end to be more comfortable discussing Dostoevsky, Joyce, and above all Shakespeare, than doing just about anything else. And it is here that a much humbler type of activity is under way, since Girard's approach to literary texts is not much more than the application of two common-sense principles.

First, great literature refers us to the 'real world', and should be taken seriously as a commentary on the conflicts and passions of real people and real societies. Secondly, the most articulate critic of a writer will be the writer himself, looking back from a standpoint of mature and tranquil reflection, so that the later works of Shakespeare or Camus can and should be used as a critical guide to the earlier ones.

One has to ask whether such an approach amounts to a 'theory' at all. It draws us once again to the question as to what kind of a body of knowledge we have here, which startles us with its mixture of psychology, anthropology, biblical revelation, literary-critical judgement. Does Girard offer a 'system' which floodlights the whole of human reality with a searing white light, or is this not rather an anti-systematic array of carefully angled spotlights illuminating particular texts and situations – this novel or that play, a historical chronicle, a newspaper article, an Amnesty International report? Where is the authentic contribution of Girard's version of mimetic theory to be found: is it in the earthquake and whirlwind of his evangelical clarion call in the face of both modernity and post-modernity – his heroic 'voyage to the end of the sciences of man' – or should we listen out for the still small voice of his close and judicious literary readings?

I am enormously indebted for what follows to the numerous scholars and colleagues who have inspired, supported and befriended me. Foremost among these, naturally, are René Girard, and his wife Martha, and all the participants of the *Colloquium on Violence and Religion* (COV&R). A special thanks to Billy Hewett SJ, James Alison and Andrew McKenna, who all read and commented on the manuscript at very short notice. It will not take a very close reading to discern that this introduction to the thought of Girard is especially indebted to two fine 'models': James Williams' *The Girard Reader* (1996), and Wolfgang Palaver's introduction, *René Girards mimetische Theorie* (2003); my heartfelt thanks to both. I also wish to acknowledge my gratitude to my *Doktorvater*, Dr Joseph Laishley SJ, and to my colleagues at Heythrop College, London, and in the British Jesuit Province, for granting me the sabbatical which allowed this work to be completed. Finally, debts of love and friendship: to my family, to my Jesuit community in Garnet House, Clapham, and to the 'St Christina Group', for their unfailing love and support.

As I was completing the first draft of this book, word reached me of the sudden death of Raymund Schwager sj, on the point of retiring from the Faculty of Theology at Innsbruck. His contribution to the theological development of mimetic theory is a significant one, and I hope I have done justice to it in these pages, even if other qualities – his warmth, his tranquil wisdom and generous faith – will have to be properly recorded elsewhere. May he rest in peace.

René Girard: His Life and Career

René Girard would be the first to acknowledge the importance of biography in the shaping of any artistic or intellectual achievement, and the key facts of his own life, in so far as they have led to the birth of mimetic theory, can be set out here. He was born on Christmas Day in Avignon in 1923. His father, the city archivist, had little sympathy for Christianity, though his mother was a devout Catholic. From the age of 10 until his conversion at 36, Girard had little to do with the Church, being politically and intellectually a thinker of the Left. He studied late medieval history, more precisely manuscripts, presenting a dissertation in 1947 on the theme of 'Private Life in Avignon in the Second Half of the Fifteenth Century'. A journey to the United States in the same year, and an experience of greater academic freedom in American universities, led him to the decision to emigrate from France to America.

After further studies in history he presented (in 1950) a second doctorate at Indiana University, on 'L'opinion américaine et la France 1940–1943'. However, his earliest employment at Indiana was as a teacher of French language and literature, with subsequent posts at Duke University, Bryn Mawr College, and then Johns Hopkins University in Baltimore, where he was Professor of Literature from 1961 to 1968. In 1966, Girard was one of the organisers of a symposium entitled 'The Languages of Criticism and the Sciences of Man': with Roland Barthes, Jacques Derrida, Jacques Lacan and other important critical theorists in attendance, the symposium was significant for bringing these new philosophical currents onto the American academic scene. This fact is useful to bear in mind, as a corrective to the impression which we can have of Girard ploughing an idiosyncratic and lonely academic furrow. In particular, Girard found the contact with Jacques Derrida of especial importance for his own theory of the scapegoat.

Girard was at State University of New York before returning to Johns Hopkins in 1976. From 1980 until his retirement in 1995 he was the Andrew Hammond Professor of French Language, Literature and Civilization at Stanford University in California. As Williams (1996) points out, Stanford University was certainly a prestigious location for Girard to find himself, but by the same token it was a centre for the kind of academic political correctness which has been inimical to Girard's intellectual concerns. His publications in this time have covered ethnology, anthropology, psychology, mythology and theology, as well as literary criticism – even though his initial academic training, as noted above, was as a medieval historian. He still lives in Stanford, where he is married to Martha, an American. They have three children, and several grandchildren.

What, specifically, are the events in Girard's life which have caused him to take such an obsessive interest in the themes of mimesis, violence and the sacred which dominate his work? Not surprisingly, growing up as a young man in France during World War II was clearly formative. A recent study has made reference to his involvement with the French Resistance during this time. Speaking of this period, Girard recalls how impressed he was, even as a young agnostic, with the fact that those of his acquaintances who seemed most able to resist being caught up by the contagious attraction of Fascism on the one hand, and of Communism on the other, were the Young Christian Workers – perhaps a pregnant observation in the light of his later religious commitment. On several occasions Girard has spoken with some openness about his conversion while working on his first book: this was at first an intellectual conversion, then more properly religious, leading to his return to Christianity at Easter 1959.

Asked to reflect on experiences of personal marginalisation which might account for his interest in the theme of scapegoating, Girard has pointed to the feeling of discrimination he felt as a 'southerner' when he arrived in Paris, and also the impression made upon him of racism towards blacks which he discovered when he moved to the

United States, though he stresses the novels of William Faulkner in this regard, rather than direct experiences of his own. Most significant, however, is his discussion, in an interview with *Der Spiegel* in 1997, of the impact of his brother's suicide before Girard emigrated from France, and the difficulty of his family coming to terms with this tragedy without seeking to apportion 'blame'.

Beyond these events, it seems that to understand where Girard is coming from we must turn to the texts that have energised and inspired him, and with which he has resonated most profoundly: the writings of Proust, Dostoevsky, Shakespeare, and ultimately the gospels. Bridging his literary and his evangelical concerns are the anthropological and mythological investigations of his middle career, and especially classical Greek drama. *The Girard Reader* (1996) remains a valuable resource for tracing the development of his thought. As I have already suggested, it is probably most helpful to think of Girard's writing career under the following three headings; the Bibliography should be consulted for fuller details.

(i) Three key works, in which the mimetic theory takes shape:

Mensonge romantique et vérité romanesqe, Grasset, Paris, 1961 (*Deceit, Desire and the Novel: Self and Other in Literary Structure*, Johns Hopkins UP, Baltimore, 1965)

La Violence et le sacré, Grasset, Paris, 1972 (*Violence and the Sacred*, Johns Hopkins UP, Baltimore; Athlone, London, 1977)

Des Choses cachées depuis la fondation du monde, Grasset, Paris, 1978 (*Things Hidden Since the Foundation of the World*, University Press, Stanford Ca., 1987. Research undertaken in collaboration with Jean-Michel Oughourlian and Guy Lefort.)

(ii) Books in which the mimetic theory is applied to specific authors or texts:

Dostoievski: Du double à l'unité, Plon, Paris, 1963 (*Resurrection from the Underground: Feodor Dostoevsky*, Crossroad, New York, 1997)

'To double business bound': Essays on Literature, Mimesis and Anthropology, Johns Hopkins UP, Baltimore; Athlone, London, 1978

Le Bouc émissaire, Grasset, Paris, 1982 (*The Scapegoat*, Johns Hopkins UP, Baltimore; Athlone, London, 1986)

La Route antique des hommes pervers; Essais sur Job, Grasset, Paris, 1985
(*Job: the victim of his people*, Athlone, London, 1987)
A Theatre of Envy: William Shakespeare, Oxford University Press, 1991
Je vois Satan tomber comme l'éclair, Grasset, Paris, 1999 (*I See Satan Fall like Lightning*, Maryknoll, New York, 2001)

(iii) Important interviews, conference presentations, etc.:

'To double business bound': Essays on Literature, Mimesis and Anthropology, Johns Hopkins UP, Baltimore; Athlone, London, 1978, including Girard's interview from *Diacritics* 8 (1978)

Assmann, H. (ed.), *Sobre idolos y sacrifios: René Girard con teologos de la liberacion*, Coleccion Economia – teologia, 1991

Adams, R., 'A Conversation with René Girard: Interview by Rebecca Adams', *Religion and Literature* 25.2, Notre Dame Indiana, 1993

Quand ces choses commenceront . . . Entretiens avec Michel Treguer, arléa, Paris, 1994

Celui par qui le scandale arrive, Desclée de Brouwer, Paris, 2001, including an interview with Maria Stella Barberi

CHAPTER 1

Desire is Mimetic

CHAPTER SUMMARY

1. The theory of human interrelations referred to as René Girard's 'mimetic theory' has at its origin a 'conversion' experience, a movement towards enlightenment which Girard discovered in the lives and work of five selected European novelists. This conversion is more explicitly Christian in some cases (e.g. Dostoevsky) than in others (e.g. Proust or Stendhal). It is nevertheless inseparable from motifs and symbols of religious transcendence, such as worship, idolatry, communion, death and resurrection.

2. Each of these novelists explores the truth that 'desire is mimetic'. By this Girard affirms, first of all, that human desire is to be distinguished from need or appetite, in so far as appetites are biologically preconditioned, whereas desire is much more a function of culture. Human biological needs (hunger, thirst) are straightforward and easily identified; the objects of desire are much harder to specify, being potentially unlimited and infinitely varied.

3. For this reason, men and women learn from one another what it is they should desire. In this respect, humans are 'mimetic', they copy one another not just in terms of language, gestures and other external attributes, but also in terms of what they desire. Mimetic theory therefore challenges and rejects the idea of the desiring self as autonomous and independent – 'the Romantic Lie'. By contrast, Girard's chosen novelists deal with the 'novelistic truth' concerning the instability of the desiring self. This theme is especially manifested in the drama of Shakespeare, for example in *A Midsummer Night's Dream*.

4. Where mimesis leads to a convergence of desires upon the same object – as with the example of children arguing over toys – the result will often be rivalry, and possibly outright conflict. Desire orientated towards the possession of objects is referred to as 'acquisitive' mimesis. Where desire is directed beyond objects at some less specific, quasi-transcendent state of well-being or fulfilment, it is known as 'metaphysical' desire.

[handwritten: give example. Example: JAZZ piece is a He's Doult]

[handwritten: Look Though articles & media for the Two desires]

drew

5. The mediated nature of desire can best be illustrated as a triangle, i.e. as a relation between subject – model – object. The potential for rivalry and conflict between subject and model depends on the distance between them (the height of the triangle): where the distance between subject and model is greater, so that there is no danger of them coming into rivalry (either because the model is a fictional character, or because there are adequate social or cultural barriers between them), then Girard speaks of 'external' mediation. Where subject and model occupy the same social space and are capable of entering into competition with one other, we have the more dangerous, 'internal' mediation.

6. Girard sees in the development of the novel from Cervantes to Dostoevsky a progression from external to internal mediation. This is to be linked to socio-cultural factors, in Europe's development towards democratic equality, and the breaking down of hierarchically stratified societies. Implicit in the analysis of the novelists, therefore, is a theory about modernity.

Scott Cowdell's New Book.

7. Two philosophical themes are important, as background to Girard's insights regarding mimetic desire. Kojève's reading of Hegel's *Phenomenology of Spirit* is influential, notably the desire for recognition and the Master–Slave dialectic. Similarly, there are clear affinities between Girard's argument and Max Scheler's account of *ressentiment*, especially as both are engaging with Nietzsche's critique of Christianity. At the same time, Girard differs from Scheler and Hegel in important respects.

book

Bring

Desire is Mimetic

Girard's theory begins with a realisation of the importance of mimesis in human desire, a conviction that he arrived at while working on his first book, *Deceit, Desire and the Novel* in 1959. So we need to start with an explanation of what he understands by 'mimesis'.

The five novelists whom Girard considers in this book deal with nothing less than 'the collapse of the autonomous self'. The first and perhaps clearest example of what this means is Don Quixote, whom we will turn to shortly. As mentioned in the Introduction, however, this literary study was accompanied by a 'collapse' of an immediate kind for Girard himself, or at least a profound shake-up of his beliefs and values. In an interview he tells how he approached this study 'in the pure demystification mode: cynical, destructive, very much in the spirit of the atheist intellectuals of the time'. Such an attitude of 'debunking', however, can eventually turn back on itself. If all one finds in other people is inauthenticity and bad faith, something very like the religious concept of original sin will emerge into view: 'An experience of demystification, if radical enough, is very close to an experience of conversion.' Girard saw that the lives of a number of great writers manifest precisely this pattern, and by the time he came to write the last chapter of the book, he realised that he was undergoing his own version of the experience he was describing. This caused him to return to reading the gospels, and to acknowledge that he had now become a Christian.

Girard stresses that this was as yet only an intellectual-literary conversion, and a fairly comfortable one. When he had a health scare in early 1959, namely the discovery of a cancerous spot on his forehead, the issue became much more existential. His conversion was now a genuinely religious one, and he returned to the Catholic Church during Lent of that year, in time for a 'real Easter experience, a death and resurrection experience'. He describes himself now as 'an ordinary Christian'.

Here, then, is the key to understanding the writers under consideration in *Deceit, Desire and the Novel*. In spite of their diverse backgrounds and religious affiliations, they have in common an experience of conversion, which is also to be thought of as a 'death and resurrection experience'. For the authors themselves, this experience of collapse and recovery may be implicitly or explicitly religious. For Girard, the kind of event that he is describing (whether it is understood religiously or not) is so pivotal to their works, that he takes it to be constitutive of the genre we call the 'novel'. He therefore sets up a contrast between 'novel' and 'romance'; the novel tells us the truth about human desire, whereas romantic literature perpetuates only untruth about the autonomy and stability of human desire.

The first author considered in *Deceit, Desire and the Novel* is Miguel Cervantes, the creator of Don Quixote. Quixote has decided that he wishes to be a knight errant. He has decided upon this as a result of reading courtly literature, and he explains to his servant, Sancho Panza, why he has chosen to take as his model Amadis de Gaul, the most prominent of the literary heroes he has been reading about:

> I want you to know, Sancho, that the famous Amadis of
> Gaul was one of the most perfect knight errants. But what

am I saying, one of the most perfect? I should say the only, the first, the unique, the master and lord of all those who existed in the world . . . when a painter wants to become famous for his art he tries to imitate the originals of the best masters he knows . . . In the same way Amadis was the pole, the star, the sun, for brave and amorous knights, and we others who fight under the banner of love and chivalry should imitate him. Thus, my friend Sancho, I reckon that whoever imitates him best will come closest to perfect chivalry.

(*Don Quixote*, cited in Girard, 1965, p. 1)

By allowing this fictional character to choose for him all the things he should desire, Don Quixote effectively abandons any independent judgement of his own. He has no independent 'self'. Girard illustrates this state of affairs geometrically, by declaring that desire has a *triangular* structure. Instead of desire being a single linear relation (subject A desires object B – 'Quixote desires to be a perfect knight'), we have three elements: A only desires B because C (in this case, Amadis de Gaul) has directed his attention towards it. Since Quixote's desires are channelled or mediated by Amadis, point C of the triangle is called the 'mediator' or 'model'.

Cervantes is not the first writer to consider the theme of mimesis, of course. A long Western philosophical tradition has followed Aristotle in the *Poetics* – 'man is distinguished from other life-forms by his capacity for imitation'. All human learning, and especially the acquisition of language, takes place through imitation. What Girard insists has been neglected is an understanding of imitation which is expansive enough to include *desire*. Not just language and external gestures, but desire is also conditioned by our imitative human nature. Girard notes that some writers are inexplicably ambiguous or hostile towards mimesis; for example, no satisfactory explanation has been offered as to why Plato (*Republic*, Book 10) considers mimesis to be dangerous or problematic, and it is precisely this mystery which Girard thinks he has solved. Before seeing why this might be so, we may first consider another description of mimesis, offered by J. M. Oughourlian, a psychiatrist and collaborator with Girard:

Just as in the cosmos, the planets, stars, and galaxies are simultaneously held together and kept apart by gravity, so also mimesis keeps human beings together and apart, assuring at one and the same time the *cohesion* of the social fabric and the relative *autonomy* of the members that make it up. In physics, it is the force of attraction, gravity, that holds bodies together in space. They would be pitilessly hurled against each other into a final fusion if gravity did not also preserve their autonomy, and hence their existence, through motion. In psychology, the movement of mimesis that renders one autonomous and relatively individual is called 'desire' . . . I have always thought that what one customarily calls the 'I' or 'self' in psychology is an unstable, constantly changing, evanescent structure. I think, to evoke the intuitions of Hegel on this point, that only desire brings this self into existence. Because desire is the only psychological motion, it alone, it seems to me, is capable of producing the self and breathing life into it. The first hypothesis that I would like to formulate in this regard is this: *desire gives rise to the self and, by its movement, animates it.* The second hypothesis, which I have adopted unreservedly since I first became aware of it, is that *desire is mimetic.*

(J. M. Oughourlian, 1991, pp. 11–12)

This model of universal gravitation is memorable and easily understood, and neatly refers us back to Quixote's description of Amadis as 'the pole, the star, the sun', for anyone who wishes to be a perfect knight. It even hints at the way we speak about modern celebrity culture – the 'stars' and 'megastars' who populate the world of entertainment, media and sport are the focus of seemingly infinite fascination for mere ordinary human beings, so that we speak of their 'pulling power' at the box office, their rising and falling, and so on. Also, the planetary model sums up well the spirit of Girard's whole enterprise. Girard insists that with the idea of mimesis he has hit upon a simple but key organising idea, one which will transform our way of thinking about the human sciences, just as the theories of gravity and evolution have drastically altered our understanding of physics and biology.

Lastly, this models alerts us to the darker side of desire. 'Mimesis keeps human beings together and apart.' As well as attraction, there _the liberal world of P.C._

is repulsion. As we have seen from the Introduction, Girard's investigation of desire relates to a wider question: why, of all life-forms in creation, are humans apparently the most violent and prone to conflict? Girard wishes to distance himself, on the one hand, from theorists who posit an aggressive drive or instinct as the source of human conflicts. One reason for his disagreement is that Girard is working with a distinction between _needs or appetites_, which are 'natural', on the one hand, and _desire_, which is much more conditioned by culture and social interaction, on the other.

A second type of theory against which Girard is reacting is the romantic or liberal celebration of desire _per se_, according to which all human distress and negativity is an effect of the distortion of natural desire by external forces. The cause of conflict and aggression is located outside of the self, either in alienating social conditions, or in a repressive father-figure, and so on. If the external factor is removed, the self is 'liberated' to express its desires unhindered. As the description offered by Oughourlian implies, this conception of the self as an autonomous unit is now being widely questioned by philosophers. Girard and others refer polemically to it as 'the Romantic Lie'. The self is, rather, 'an unstable, constantly changing, evanescent structure', brought into existence by desire.

St Augustine expresses this theologically: 'Lord, our hearts are restless, till they rest in Thee!' The fact is, people do not know what they want – therefore they imitate the desire of others. We need only reflect upon the vast expenditure and creativity which goes into advertising – a medium, incidentally, which is becoming ever more forthright about its own mimetic strategies. Recent examples include the slogan in a major English department store, which declared unashamedly: 'You want it – you buy it – you forget it!', while my own favourite is a poster selling jeans, in which a scantily clad model scowls defiantly over the slogan: 'No one tells me what to wear!' In fact, any kind of market is nothing other than a mechanism for the harmonious mediation of desires. If we think of a currency market where everyone wants to buy euros, my 'desire' will be to buy euros also. As soon as the market switches to dollars, my own preference will 'mysteriously' change accordingly. A number of economic theorists have in fact attempted to utilise mimetic theory in their analyses of market behaviour.

From an evolutionary perspective, the mimetic adoption of

says Christianity is siding against the forces of repression (chaos)

When I was a "psycho therapist" I did a great deal of Thinking on "the theory of the self!"

another's desire has replaced instinctual behaviour as the prime determinant of human action. This is part of Girard's explanation of why humans seem to be much more prone to deadly conflict than other life-forms. The instinctual 'braking' mechanisms which will normally prevent an escalation of conflict among animals, for example, are not present for humans. As if this were not worrying enough, the convergence of two or more desires upon the same object has, inevitably, a potential for conflict. Girard summarises as follows:

> We find ourselves reverting to an ancient notion – mimesis – one whose conflictual implications have always been misunderstood. We must understand that desire itself is essentially mimetic, directed toward an object desired by the model.
>
> The mimetic quality of childhood desire is universally recognized. Adult desire is virtually identical, except that (most strikingly in our own culture) the adult is generally ashamed to imitate others for fear of revealing his lack of being. The adult likes to assert his independence and to offer himself as a model to others; he invariably falls back on the formula 'Imitate me!' in order to conceal his own lack of originality.
>
> Two desires converging on the same object are bound to clash. Thus, mimesis coupled with desire leads automatically to conflict. However, humans always seem half blind to this conjunction, unable to perceive it as a cause of rivalry. In human relationships words like 'sameness' and 'similarity' evoke an image of harmony. If we have the same tastes and like the same things, surely we are bound to get along. But what will happen when we share the same desires? Only the major dramatists and novelists have partly understood and explored this form of rivalry.
>
> (Girard, 1977, p. 146)

As long as the object of yearning is not closed off to general use – for example, if my friend and I want to learn the same language, or read the same book, or listen to the same piece of music – then conflict need not arise. But as soon as the object is cordoned off from this possibility of shared enjoyment, as is the case with sexual relationships, or jockeying for social prestige, mimesis will lead to competition. Once the desiring subject wants to possess the object for him or herself, the person who first brought the desired object to recognition becomes a rival and an obstacle. One word which Girard uses to describe the model who has become a rival is the biblical Greek word *skandalon*, scandal, or 'stumbling block'.

Two hands reach, not quite simultaneously, for the same object. The outcome is bitter rivalry, even outright conflict.

It is striking how often this simple formula or image is used by Girard, especially with reference to children. He often cites the example of children playing in a roomful of toys, when an argument breaks out because two or more infants want to play with the same toy, even though there are plenty to go round. To repeat, desire possesses a *triangular* structure. Along the base of the triangle we find the desiring subject (who is also the imitator), and the desired object. At the apex of the triangle we have the model, the one who has indicated in the first place that the object is desirable.

It is also worth noting that the model/obstacle/rival need not in fact be an actual person. In fact, in three of the novelists considered by Girard, mimetic passions are aroused by the subject's reading of fictional literature. Don Quixote imitates a fictional hero, Amadis de Gaul, as we have seen. Similarly in Flaubert: when Madame Bovary embarks on the first of her adulterous affairs, she recalls ecstatically the romantic literature which had nourished her desires up to that point:

> Then she caught sight of herself in the mirror, and was amazed by the way she looked. Never had her eyes been so enormous, so dark, so deep: her whole being was transfigured by some subtle emanation.
>
> 'I have a lover! I have a lover!' she kept repeating to herself, reveling in the thought as though she were beginning a second puberty. At last she was going to know the joys of love, the fever of the happiness she had despaired of. She was entering a marvelous realm where all would be passion, ecstasy, rapture: she was in the midst of an endless blue expanse, scaling the glittering heights of passion; everyday life had receded, and lay far below, in the shadows between those peaks.

> She remembered the heroines of novels she had read, and the lyrical legion of those adulterous women began to sing in her memory with sisterly voices that enchanted her. Now she saw herself as one of those *amoureuses* whom she had so envied: she was becoming, in reality, one of that gallery of fictional figures; the long dream of her youth was coming true. She was full of a delicious sense of vengeance. How she had suffered! But now her hour of triumph had come; and love, so long repressed, was gushing forth in joyful effervescence. She savoured it without remorse, without anxiety, without distress.
>
> (Flaubert, *Madame Bovary*, p. 153)

This link between reading and desire is also made explicit by the narrator in Marcel Proust's *A La Recherche du Temps Perdu*: 'But I was incapable of seeing a thing unless a desire to do so had been aroused in me by reading . . . I knew how often I had been unable to give my attention to things or to people, whom afterwards, once their image had been presented to me in solitude by an artist, I would have gone leagues and risked death to rediscover.' As Girard points out, the printed word has a magical power of suggestion for the young Marcel, evident in his adulation of the writer Bergotte, and extending even to the theatrical posters he reads on the Champs-Elysées.

To complete this initial survey of mimetic desire, we should add two further considerations. We have seen that Girard posits a triangular structure for desire: the subject's desire for an object is mediated by that of the model, so that A desires B because C desires it. However, it is not strictly true that the subject always desires an 'object' at all. What really drives the individual may be something much more elusive and imprecise: the search for a quasi-transcendent state of well-being, of fulfilment, of self-actualisation, which goes beyond simple possession of any object or set of objects. Girard notes this distinction by referring to two kinds or degrees of mimetic desire: one is 'acquisitive' mimesis, where the desire is centred on a specific object (the child's toy, for example), and the second is 'metaphysical desire', where no specific object is aimed at, but rather an indeterminate but insistent yearning for the fullness of 'being'.

Secondly, we have seen that Girard talks about a 'conversion' experience which his chosen novelists experience (even though this does not necessarily involve an explicit religious adherence on the part of the author concerned). Girard considers this experience to be crucial to the effectiveness of the novel *genre*. He contrasts 'novel' and 'romance' as types of literature which, respectively, reveal the truth about (mimetic) desire, and perpetuate the 'Romantic Lie' about desire's autonomy. The Czech writer Milan Kundera, in his *Theory of the Novel*, has written appreciatively of Girard's treatment of mimetic desire. Girard quotes Kundera as saying that mimetic desire is the distillation of 'a particular kind of wisdom', which contemporary culture and instrumental reason has difficulty in recognising (Assmann, 1996, p. 289). Kundera's most important novel, *The Joke,* in fact lends itself very well to a Girardian analysis, since the plot centres on the humiliating public 'scapegoating' of the protagonist by a zealous Communist tribunal.

When Desire Turns Ugly

In the second part of this chapter, we will expand and deepen our understanding of Girard's discovery of mimetic desire, most especially concerning its darker or conflictual aspects. As well as the novelists whom Girard has been considering, such as Cervantes and Dostoevsky, another important literary source needs to be introduced. Not for the last time in this book, I will refer to Girard's use of Shakespeare in order to illustrate his theory, in particular his collection of essays entitled *A Theatre of Envy: William Shakespeare* (1991). Girard himself stresses the significance of the dramatist for his entire project, when he writes in the Introduction to that book: 'My work on Shakespeare is inextricably linked to everything I ever wrote, beginning with an essay on five European novelists.' This is quite a large claim, so we must see what it entails.

The argument of *A Theatre of Envy* is that Shakespeare, early in his career, made precisely the same discovery as Girard – that desire is mimetically configured, though Shakespeare uses his own terminology: 'suggested desire', 'jealous desire', 'emulation', and above all, 'envy'. As his dramatic career progresses, Shakespeare not only learns to present more and more complex versions of this phenomenon, he does so in such a way that they can stand alongside the more standard 'non-mimetic', that is, more popular, interpretations of the plays. The challenge Shakespeare sets himself, according to Girard, is to write about emulation and so forth, but in an indirect or hidden fashion, so as to appeal to different levels of sophistication in his audience. Girard notes, wryly: 'As for Shakespeare, he quickly realized that to wave mimetic desire like a red flag in front of the public is not the sure road to success (as I myself have never managed to learn, I suppose)' (1991, p. 4).

The plays which most attract Girard's attention are *A Midsummer Night's Dream,* and *Troilus and Cressida.* Before this, the basic mimetic pattern is set out in *Two Gentlemen of Verona,* in which two very close friends become rivals, because they have aroused in each other a passion for the same girl. In *A Midsummer Night's Dream,* the treatment of this same theme is more sophisticated and effective. Of the 38 chapters in *A Theatre of Envy,* six deal with scenes from this play alone: Girard rates it so highly as an exposition of mimetic desire that he declares it should be 'compulsory reading for anthropologists'. According to Girard's mimetic reading of the *Dream,* the classic notion of stable and autonomous love – what we have been calling 'the Romantic Lie' – is ruthlessly and persistently held up to ridicule. The plot centres on two pairs of lovers whose relationships become entangled, so that the young men fall hopelessly in love with each of the girls in turn, at the same time.

Why does this happen, and why should erotic wires get crossed in this way? One of the lovers, Lysander, does famously declare that 'for aught that ever I could read/ Could ever hear by tale or history/ The course of true love never did run smooth'. (Yet again, we have someone bowing to the authority of fictional literary examples, in order to declaim what 'true love' is like!) Lysander is saying that the barriers traditionally placed in the way of true lovers have always been imposed from *outside*: either parental opposition (as it appears so threateningly at the beginning of the play), or disparity of age or social status, or simply fate (if we think of the 'star-crossed lovers' in *Romeo and Juliet*). Beneath this luxuriant verbiage lies the shaky syllogism which Shakespeare is keen to question: 'these fictional true lovers all endured hardships; we too are having to endure hardships; therefore we must be true lovers'.

As it happens, the plans of the lovers in the *Dream* are sent awry, not by any of these imposing obstacles, but by a bunch of incompetent and mischievous fairies who are a little too clumsy with their love potion. The play can be enjoyed on this child-like level, but if we read the play as grown-ups, says Girard, Shakespeare is really presenting before our eyes the volatility of mimetic desire. (When Puck declares at the end of the play: 'And Jack shall have Jill', he is being particularly sardonic.) We must not take these tripping fairies too seriously: this is an adult play, the roots and causes of the lovers' discords are to be found within and among themselves, and nowhere else.

To return, however, to the analysis as it unfolds in *Deceit, Desire and the Novel*. So far we have looked in general at the mechanics of mimetic desire, which are to be found as a common feature in the writers Girard has selected. The true significance of this discovery can only be appreciated, however, when we look at the differences between the authors as well as their similarities. The five writers are not quite placed in chronological order, according to which Proust should come after Dostoevsky (we shall see later why Girard swaps them round), but we have a general survey of the novel, spanning the modern period from the early seventeenth to the twentieth centuries. Each writer configures the theme of mimetic desire differently, Girard maintains, because extreme mimetic pressures and influences make themselves increasingly felt during the modern period, pressures which are manifest in the social interactions recorded in his chosen novels.

Rather than look successively at Cervantes, Flaubert, Stendhal, Proust and Dostoevsky, let us examine the argument by comparing the first and last of these. On the face of it, Cervantes' character Don Quixote and the tormented heroes and anti-heroes of Dostoevsky's novels seem to occupy different planets. *Don Quixote*, we have always thought, is a comic tale of a misguided buffoon, who embarks on ludicrous adventures, but thankfully comes to no harm. The reason is the hierarchical relationship between the model and the imitator. Because the model is a fictional character, there can never be a rivalrous conflict between Don Quixote and Amadis; the gap between them cannot be transgressed. In the same way, the social distance between Don Quixote and his acknowledged pupil and servant, Sancho Panza, prevents any conflict between them. The novel ends without violence.

This 'safe' form of mimesis is called 'external mediation' or 'external mimesis'. As long as social differences or other distinctions are able to channel mimetic desire, the conflictual potential of mimetic desire is never actualised. This can be expressed once again by means of the triangle which is the principal geometric figure of mimetic desire: if we think of an isosceles triangle, with the model or mediator at its apex, then degrees of mediation can be expressed in terms of the distance between the apex and the base. In 'safe', external mediation, we have a tall triangle, with a clear distance between mediator and subject. If the triangle is made more squat, then we have the more perilous situation of 'internal mediation', where the subject and model are, literally, too close for comfort.

In Dostoevsky, we have just such a triangular pattern. The characters move on the same social level, and we are confronted with a much more frenzied world of destructive mimetic interaction – culminating in the alleged father-murder in *The Brothers Karamazov*. Here we find a rivalistic desire between individuals, frenziedly struggling for the same social space. Meet 'Underground Man':

> 'I am a sick man . . . I am an angry man. I am an unattractive man. I think there is something wrong with my liver . . .'

The speaker is the unnamed, splenetic anti-hero of *Notes from Underground,* whom Dostoevsky describes as 'this real man of the Russian majority'. He is a petty bureaucrat, a man consumed by a ferocious obsession with other people's opinion of him, who finds himself nauseated by the company of his peers at the same time as he is hopelessly fascinated and attracted by them. He spends months considering how to get revenge on an army officer who has publicly humiliated him. Later, in a richly comic scene, the Underground Man drunkenly gate-crashes a banquet of former school companions, now army officers and civil servants like himself, whom he loathes and despises, yet whose company he cannot bear to be without. He exasperates and offends by his presence, like a moth crashing continuously into a lamp:

> Smiling scornfully, I paced backwards and forwards on the side of the room opposite the sofa, along the wall from the table to the stove and back. I was trying with all my might to show that I could do without them; meanwhile I purposely made a clatter with my boots, coming down hard

on the heels. But it was all in vain; they didn't even notice. I had the patience to walk about straight in front of them in this fashion from eight o'clock till eleven, always in the same track, from the table to the stove and from the stove back again to the table: 'I am walking to please myself and nobody can stop me.' . . . To humiliate oneself more shamelessly and wilfully was impossible, and this I fully, all too fully understood, yet all the same I continued to pace from the table to the stove and back. 'Oh, if only you know what thoughts and emotions I am capable of, and how enlightened I am!' I thought sometimes, turning in imagination to the sofa where my enemies sat. But my enemies acted as though I wasn't even in the room. Once, and only once, they turned towards me, and that was when Zverkov began to talk about Shakespeare and I let out a sudden contemptuous laugh. It was such a vilely artificial snort that they all ceased talking at once and silently watched me for about two minutes, attentively and seriously, as I walked along the wall from the table to the stove, *without paying them the slightest attention*. But nothing happened; they did not speak to me and after two minutes they ignored me again.

Compare this passage with Proust's description (from *Within a Budding Grove*, quoted in *Things Hidden*, p. 301) of holiday-makers, strolling by the sea at Balbec:

> All these people . . . pretending not to see, so as to let it be thought that they were not interested in them, but covertly eyeing, for fear of running into them, the people who were walking beside or coming towards them, did in fact bump into them, became entangled with them, because each was mutually the object of the same secret attention veiled beneath the same apparent disdain.

Girard draws on another story by Dostoevsky, *The Eternal Husband*. The 'eternal husband' of the title is Trousotsky, whose wife has just died. She had had two lovers, one of whom also dies: Trousotsky attends his funeral procession, where he displays quite extravagant grief. The widower then attaches himself in the most bizarre fashion to the other lover, Veltschaninoff, with whom he is clearly fascinated. He visits him uninvited in the middle of the night, drinks his health, kisses him on the lips . . . in short, his wife's lover has become his model, mediator and obstacle. Trousotsky moves round him like a planet circling the sun.

The plot becomes even more bizarre when Trousotsky falls in love again, and declares that he wishes to remarry. He asks Veltschaninoff to help him choose a present for his beloved, and even to accompany him on a visit to her. The predictable happens: Veltschaninoff easily charms his way into the affections of the fiancée and her family, so that Trousotsky himself is now totally disregarded.

This looks like the most masochistic kind of behaviour; in fact, the Eternal Husband is incapable of loving someone unless his choice has been ratified and approved by his model-rival. Veltschaninoff is an accomplished 'Don Juan', and without his seal of approval, the girl will appear to be worthless to Trousotsky. He yearns to be like, or even to surpass, his rival, to have his success with women, but because he only encounters failure he can never escape from Veltschaninoff's influence. The triangularity of the Eternal Husband's desire is reaffirmed at the end of the novel, when the narrator (who is Veltschaninoff himself) meets Trousotsky, years later, together with his charming new wife . . . in the company of a dashing young officer. As Girard observes in his later book on Dostoevsky: 'Masochists are always fascinated artisans of their own unhappiness':

> Why does [Trousotsky] rush into his own humiliation? Because he is immensely vain and proud. This response is paradoxical only in appearance. When Trousotsky discovers that his wife prefers another man to him, the shock he experiences is dreadful because he makes it a duty to be the center and navel of the universe. The man is a former serf owner; he is rich. He lives in a world of masters and slaves and is incapable of envisaging a middle term between these two extremes; the least failure condemns him to servitude. A deceived husband, he pledges himself to being a sexual zero. After having thought of himself as someone from whom power and success naturally radiat-

ed, he now sees himself as human waste from whom impotence and ridicule inevitably ooze.

(Girard, 1997, p. 49)

It should be clear from these two stories alone that the Russian novelist offers very striking expositions of the most extreme kind of mimetic interaction, which justifies Girard putting Dostoevsky at the climax of *Deceit, Desire and the Novel*. Because the distance between hero and model has been shortened, the potential for both morbid fascination, and for rivalry and violence, is intensified.

The contrast between mimetic interaction in Cervantes and Dostoevsky is like day and night. And yet both writers, according to Girard, are seeking to illustrate the same psychological mechanism: mimetic desire. Why, then, is there such a shocking difference between them?

One answer is to look at the social and cultural differences which set the seventeenth-century writer apart from the nineteenth-century one. This period sees the erosion of precisely those hierarchical boundaries which prevented Quixote and Sancho Panza from coming into conflict. We alluded to this in Girard's distinction between 'external' and 'internal' mediation. In this increased potentiality of mimetic desire from Cervantes to Dostoevsky is mirrored the development of our modern world, a world in which long-established differentiation is eroded in the face of equality and democracy. Mimesis therefore encounters fewer and fewer barriers; in place of external mediation we have more and more internal. This world is characterised by intense competition, rivalry, envy and jealousy.

Thomas Hobbes' *Leviathan* puts forward a diagnosis of this condition. The problem begins, for Hobbes, with the competitive nature of the modern world, and its unavoidable logic of acquisitive mimesis. In Chapter 13 of *Leviathan*, 'Of the Naturall Condition of Mankind, as concerning their Felicity, and Misery', he wrote:

> From this equality of ability, ariseth equality of hope in the attaining of our Ends. And therefore if any two men desire the same thing, which nevertheless they cannot both enjoy, they become enemies; and in the way to their End, (which is principally their owne conservation, and sometimes their delectation only,) endeavour to destroy, or subdue one an other . . . Againe, men have no pleasure,

(but on the contrary a great deale of griefe) in keeping company, where there is no power able to over-awe them all. For every man looketh that his companion should value him, at the same rate he sets upon himselfe . . . so that in the nature of man, we find three principall causes of quarrell. First, Competition; Secondly, Diffidence; Thirdly, Glory.

By 'diffidence', Hobbes means the wariness which people show towards each other, precisely because they are of equal ability, with no one noticeably stronger than the others. This diffidence is at the same time a source of self-assertion, since each desires the esteem or 'recognition' of the others. As Hobbes memorably describes just after this passage, this means that the 'natural' state of humanity is one of all-pervasive warfare, a theme we will look at in the next chapter.

According to Girard, these mimetic pressures build up intolerably, so that by the nineteenth century the disease has its own name: the Underground Man and Trousotsky, along with numerous other Dostoevskian heroes, are suffering from *ressentiment*. The French word is preferable to the English 'resentment', because it conveys better this sense of emotional ricochet, where the affective life of the hero is borrowed from or dictated by someone else – with turbulent consequences.

Perhaps a more familiar example here would be the character of Antonio Salieri in Peter Schaffer's play and film, *Amadeus*. The play is about the life of Mozart as told from the perspective of Salieri, the imperial court composer. He has dedicated his life and music to God, only to find himself confronted in rivalry by a dissolute yet brilliant genius. The comparison is a disastrous one: Salieri, now convinced that God is mocking him, renounces his piety and determines to frustrate God's purposes by destroying his 'creature'. At the close of the drama, Salieri (incarcerated in an asylum because of his jealous obsession) declaims himself to be the 'patron saint of mediocrity'. More accurately, he ranks alongside the Eternal Husband and the Underground Man as one of the patron saints of *ressentiment*.

Philosophical Background

Up to now, the first phase of mimetic theory – the discovery that desire is mimetic – has been presented through Girard's reading of key novelists and of Shakespearean drama. The remainder of this chapter will examine his theory against the background of other philosophical approaches to the same theme. It is clear that existentialist writers such as Sartre and Camus are very influential for Girard, but two other texts will be considered here, as a way of sharpening up the distinctive claims of mimetic theory: Hegel's *Phenomenology of Spirit* (as interpreted by Kojève), and Max Scheler's *Ressentiment*.

Hegel's *Phenomenology of Spirit* deals with two themes which are of significance for Girard's project: the desire for recognition (*Anerkennung*), and the Master–Slave dialectic. The 'version' of Hegel which concerns us is the interpretation given by Alexander Kojève, in a famous series of lectures in Paris between 1933 and 1939, which excited and influenced a generation of important thinkers, including Hannah Arendt, George Bataille, Maurice Merleau-Ponty, and Jacques Lacan. René Girard read the text of Kojève's lectures as he was writing *Deceit, Desire and the Novel* in 1959.

Like Girard, Hegel gives an important role to desire in the formation of the self. His argument, as summarised by Kojève, runs as follows. Hegel's statement that 'the human is self-consciousness' requires a view of the subject that goes beyond Descartes' 'I think therefore I am'; the human is more than just a *thinking* subject. In order to be able to say 'I', a subject must have desire, and this has to be a desire for a non-natural object, if man is to transcend his animal nature. For Hegel, the only possible candidate for such an object is *the desire of another*. This means, to be recognised by the other person, to place oneself as the object of someone else's desire. Self-consciousness, for Hegel, is a function of the desire for recognition:

> Desire is human – or, more exactly, 'humanizing,' 'anthropogenetic' – only provided that it is directed toward another *Desire* and an *other* Desire. To be *human*, man must act not for the sake of subjugating a *thing*, but for the sake of subjugating another *Desire* (for the thing). The man who desires a thing humanly acts not so much to possess the *thing* as to make another *recognize* his *right* – as will be said later – to that thing, to make another recognize him as the *owner* of the thing. And he does this – in the final analysis – in order to make the other recognize his

superiority over the other. It is only Desire of such a Recognition (*Anerkennung*), it is only Action that flows from such a desire, that creates, realizes, and reveals a *human*, non-biological I.

(Kojève, p. 40)

The subject's desire for recognition is so overwhelming that he is prepared to fight for it, even to the death – as are all the other competing subjects, similarly struggling for recognition. So for Hegel, human existence is unthinkable without bloody wars for prestige, conflicts in which, paradoxically, 'man will risk his biological life to satisfy his *nonbiological* desire' (Kojève, p. 41). In fact, exactly such a struggle was going on outside Hegel's window, so to speak, as he was writing the *Phenomenology*: in 1806, Napoleon's troops were moving to encounter the Prussian army at the Battle of Jena.

Nevertheless, although the subject is prepared to struggle and lose his life, it is also the case that a struggle in which all the combatants are killed, except for the solitary victor, would be counterproductive. That victor would no longer be a *human* being, because human reality consists in the recognition of one man by another. One can only posit, therefore, a struggle in which both adversaries remain alive, but in which one yields to the other – a victor who becomes the Master of the vanquished.

'The vanquished has subordinated his human desire for recognition to the biological desire to preserve his life; this is what determines and reveals – to him and to the victor – his inferiority', while for the Master the opposite is true (p. 42). For Kojève, this Master–Slave dialectic is the key to understanding the *Phenomenology*. The Master's willingness to wager his life, and the Slave's unreadiness to do so, are what establish the hierarchy between them. However, this is not the end of the story. The Master is acknowledged as victor, but only by a slave consciousness, which is of little value to him. 'Mastery is an existential impasse' (p. 46). The Slave, on the other hand, is put to work by the Master, but precisely this work enables him, over time, to build up an independent consciousness. He works directly upon the world to transform it, and gradually becomes aware of the contradictions in his situation. The Slave, in contrast to the Master, can progress. There are three stages, or ideologies, to his progression: stoicism, scepticism and 'unhappy consciousness'; all are attempts by the Slave to reconcile his sense of freedom with the objective condition of his enslavement.

As mentioned above, Girard was reading Kojève's lectures on Hegel at the time of writing his book, and we can see a number of clear structural parallels with his own mimetic theory. Above all, the link between desire (which is mimetically structured) and conflict (the desire for recognition; the Master–Slave dialectic) is emphatically stated.

However, a number of important differences between Hegel and Girard need to be stressed. They differ above all in their understanding of desire: Hegel speaks of 'desiring the desire of the other' (in other words, I desire that the other should desire = recognise me), while Girard's mimetic theory holds that I 'desire according to the other' (my desire is directed according to what the other desires – I yearn for the same object as she does, whatever it may be). Girard also expresses misgivings about the necessary relation in Hegel between desire and destruction or negation. Hegel places violence at the centre of his system, and in effect sacralises it, so he is unable to offer a way out of the problematic of violence.

As we shall see in later chapters, Girard allows the Christian revelation, positively assessed, an increasingly prominent place in his thought. In *Deceit, Desire and the Novel* this preference is more implicit, but is nevertheless evident in his contrast of the 'Hegelian dialectic' with the 'novelistic dialectic' (that is, the process of enlightenment and conversion which he traces through the novels of Proust, Dostoevsky and the others). Hegel and Girard look as if they are talking about similar states of alienation, but there is a real difference between them. Hegel's 'Promethean' philosophy celebrates the subject's optimistic drive out of alienation and towards self-fulfilment, while the 'novelistic' imagination has seen through this dream and no longer believes it:

> Hegel's unhappy consciousness and Sartre's *projet* to be God are the outcome of a stubborn orientation to the transcendent, of an inability to relinquish religious patterns of desire when history has outgrown them. The novelistic consciousness is also unhappy because its need for transcendency has outlived the Christian faith. But

there the resemblances end. In the eyes of the novelist, modern man suffers, not because he refuses to become fully and totally aware of his autonomy, but because that awareness, whether real or illusory, is for him intolerable. The need for transcendency seeks satisfaction in the human world and leads the hero into all sorts of madness. Stendhal and Proust, even though they are unbelievers, part company at this point with Sartre and Hegel to rejoin Cervantes and Dostoevsky. Promethean philosophy sees in the Christian religion only a humanism which is still too timid for complete self-assertion. The novelist, regardless of whether he is a Christian, sees in the so-called modern humanism a subterranean metaphysics which is incapable of recognizing its own nature.

(Girard, 1965, pp. 158–9)

The 'subterranean metaphysics' to which Girard refers reintroduces the theme of *ressentiment*, exemplified as we have seen in the figure of the Underground Man in Dostoevsky (*Notes from the Underground,* incidentally, and perhaps not surprisingly, had a marked impression on Friedrich Nietzsche). A classic if idiosyncratic study, *Ressentiment,* by the German philosopher Max Scheler (first published in 1912), offers a thorough analysis of the phenomenon, which he characterises as follows:

> *Ressentiment* is a self-poisoning of the mind which has quite definite causes and consequences. It is a lasting mental attitude, caused by the systematic repression of certain emotions and affects which, as such, are normal components of human nature. Their repression leads to the constant tendency to indulge in certain kinds of value delusions and corresponding value judgments. The emotions and affects primarily concerned are revenge, hatred, malice, envy, the impulse to detract, and spite.
>
> (Scheler, p. 29)

Scheler wishes to examine the claim of Nietzsche that *ressentiment* is a source of moral judgements, and while he finds this a plausible notion, he is not convinced by Nietzsche's declaration in *On the*

Genealogy of Morals that Christian love is the most delicate 'flower of *ressentiment*'. Two passages from *Genealogy of Morals* give the flavour of Nietzsche's argument:

> The slave revolt in morals begins when *ressentiment* itself becomes creative and ordains values: the *ressentiment* of creatures to whom the real reaction, that of the deed, is denied and who find compensation in an imaginary revenge. While all noble morality grows from a triumphant affirmation of itself, slave morality from the outset says no to an 'outside', to an 'other', to a 'non-self'; and *this* no is its creative act.
>
> (First Essay, Section 10)

Nietzsche declares Christianity (ostensibly the most exalted form of loving religion) to be, in fact, the purest form of *ressentiment*, a 'farsighted, subterranean revenge'. Certainly, if Hegel presents a system that is only superficially Christian, then Nietzsche's opposition to Christianity is at least manifest. In fact, for Girard, this opposition is a fruitful one, as he takes up the challenge of Nietzsche's formulation, 'Dionysus or the Crucified'.

> But you are finding this hard to swallow? You have no eyes for something which took two thousand years to triumph? . . . But *this* is indeed what happened: from the trunk of that tree of revenge and hatred, Jewish hatred – the deepest and most sublime hatred, that is, the kind of hatred which creates ideals and changes the meaning of values, a hatred the like of which has never been on earth – from this tree grew something equally incomparable, a *new love*, the deepest and most sublime of all the kinds of love – and from what other trunk could it have grown? . . . But let no-one think that it somehow grew up as the genuine negation of that thirst for revenge, as the antithesis of Jewish hatred! No, the opposite is the case! Love grew forth from this hatred, as its crown, as its triumphant crown, spreading itself ever wider in the purest brightness and fullness of the sun, as a crown which pursued in the lofty realm of light the goals of hatred – victory, spoils, seduction – driven there by the same impulse

with which the roots of that hatred sank down ever further and more lasciviously into everything deep and evil.

(First Essay, Section 8)

Girard approves of Scheler's attempt to challenge the identification which Nietzsche makes between Christian religious sentiment and *ressentiment*. Scheler's failure to do this effectively, for Girard, arises from his inability to grasp the mimetic nature of desire; he is not able to fit the pieces together, even though he has done an admirable job of collecting them in the first place. In any case, his study of the phenomenon of *ressentiment* and of its significance for understanding the modern era, makes him a useful philosophical conversation partner in the articulation of mimetic theory.

Girard has declared that his overall project can be said to be 'against – or anti – Nietzsche', even though the German philosopher understood the uniqueness of Christianity in a way that few of his contemporaries were able to do. In an essay from 1978, entitled 'Strategies of Madness – Nietzsche, Wagner, and Dostoevsky', Girard explores the bizarre relationship between Nietzsche and Richard Wagner. Nietzsche's worship of the composer betrays a mimetic fascination no less intense than the one that held the Eternal Husband enthralled to his wife's lover, or the Underground Man to the colleagues he both despises and adores. Nietzsche's self-identification with, alternately, Dionysus and Christ, as his sanity deserts him, is a further indicator that his understanding of *ressentiment* is a knowledge which has been bought at considerable personal cost. In a 1984 essay, entitled 'Nietzsche versus the Crucified' (reprinted in the *Girard Reader*), Girard asserts:

> These later fragments [of Nietzsche's work] are the height of *ressentiment* in the sense that the final breakdown also is. Nietzsche's superiority over his century and ours may well be that he alone pushed the *ressentiment* that he shares with quite a few lesser mortals to such a height that it yielded its most virulent and significant fruit. None of Nietzsche's achievements as a thinker can be divorced from *ressentiment*, whether the subject is Wagner, the divine, or Nietzsche himself in *Ecce Homo*.
>
> (Williams, 1996, p. 246)

The question of Nietzsche, *ressentiment* and Christianity is neatly summed up as follows:

> *Ressentiment* is the interiorization of weakened vengeance. Nietzsche suffers so much from it that he mistakes it for the original and primary form of vengeance. He sees *ressentiment* not merely as the child of Christianity, which it certainly is, but also as its father which it certainly is not. (p. 252)

However, in the same essay, Girard relativises the whole problem of *ressentiment*, when he reminds us that compared to the twentieth-century threat of nuclear holocaust (and indeed, one might add, of the bloodletting that came soon enough after Nietzsche's death), '*ressentiment* and other nineteenth-century annoyances pale into insignificance'. There is such a thing as genuine, all-destructive vengeance, of which *ressentiment* is a weakened simulacrum. Only a relatively peaceful and stable society would have the leisure to concern itself with it. Had Nietzsche known the real horrors which were to come after his death, and with which his own theories would be associated, perhaps the theme of *ressentiment* would have been far less prominent in his writings.

CHAPTER 2

The Scapegoat Mechanism

CHAPTER SUMMARY

1. In *La violence et le sacré* (1972), René Girard extends the theory of inter-personal violence set out in his earlier work to a more general theory about social behaviour. He presents us with an understanding of 'the sacred' as the means by which a society's mimetic rivalry and its consequent aggression is contained.

2. What Girard describes as the 'scapegoat mechanism' has an important role in the establishment and maintenance of social order. On the cosmic level, the action of violently expelling or destroying a victim brings into being the most fundamental social and cultural distinctions, beginning with the crucial distinction between sacred and profane. Similarly, the basic divisions at the foundation of political order are seen to be related to the channelling of vio-lence, either inwards (upon a scapegoat) or outwards (upon a common enemy). Aeschylus and Shakespeare illustrate this theme.

3. The 'scapegoat mechanism' is actually a social process, which unfolds as fol-lows. When the cultural order is destabilised or endangered by the escala-tion of mimetic desire, a whole society can be plunged into crisis. The crisis threatens a war of 'all against all' as described in Thomas Hobbes' violent 'state of Nature'. In such a crisis, a collective obsession has engulfed the whole group, a kind of possession which Girard describes in terms of 'mon-strous doubles', or 'indifferentiation'.

4. This crisis cannot be resolved in the way that writers like Thomas Hobbes imply, when they posit a reasoned social contract between the combatants. Instead, according to Girard, the crisis is resolved by a realignment of the aggression, 'all against one'. A problem which arose because of mimetic inter-action is resolved in the same way: by one person, then another, and finally the whole group pointing a finger at the alleged cause of the disturbance. The group is then unified once more in the action of expelling or destroying the

victim. Or the group finds an external focus for its aggression, an 'enemy without' who similarly unites them.

5. As a result of its aggression being expended in this way, the group experiences a transcendence and harmony which seems to have come from 'outside'; the new-found harmony comes to be attributed in a mysterious way to the expelled victim, who thus acquires a 'sacred' numinosity, even a divine status. Though innocent in relation to the group, he or she is regarded after the death or expulsion as both good and evil at the same time – that is, as sacred, because he or she is seen as both instigator and resolver of the crisis. This is called a 'double transference'.

6. Key religious phenomena such as prohibitions (taboos), rituals (sacrifices) and myths all have the function of helping the community to 'contain' its mimetic violence – even if they seem to do so by contradictory means. Prohibitions cordon off or 'quarantine' the objects or behaviour which are the potential sources of conflict. By contrast, ritual (especially sacrifice) is a momentary relaxation of taboos, whereby the community allows itself an 'acceptable' dosage of violence and chaos, much as a small dose of a virus may inoculate against the disease in its more virulent form. Myths are, typically, rationalisations or disguised accounts of an original act of violence, the truth of which the group needs to conceal or displace from itself.

7. The explanation of religion which is being offered here is summarised by the declaration that 'violence is the heart and secret soul of the sacred'. By bringing together literature and myth, Girard establishes a link between mimetic desire and the victimisation (otherwise referred to as 'victimage mechanism') which constitutes a theory of religion and social origins. There is a clear correlation between this kind of explanation and that put forward by Sigmund Freud in *Totem and Taboo*, where Freud also posits a 'founding murder', but without being in a position to articulate this satisfactorily in terms of a surrogate victim.

The lives and works of five major novelists enabled René Girard to formulate his understanding that desire is mimetic. In so far as Cervantes, Flaubert and the others became aware of this anthropological fact, they experienced a kind of 'conversion': an appropriate word, since the experience is usually related in their novels by means of religious imagery and language, even though the authors themselves have very different religious allegiances. Once we have recognised that desire is mimetic, it is possible to understand why the desires of two or more people can all too easily converge on the same object. Where the object can be shared between the desiring parties, there is no problem, but if this is not the case, then rivalry can come about even (and especially) between people who up to this point have been the closest of friends, or even relations.

Girard approaches great literature by insisting that it can be a surer guide to human truth than the present-day human and social sciences. This places him in disagreement with many contemporary philosophical and aesthetic theorists, according to whom literary texts can only ever relate to other fictional texts. They should not be read as if they have any bearing on genuine ethical or religious situations. So we are confronted from the start with an important initial decision: has literature anything at all to do with the reality of human life? Can we really learn from writers like Dostoevsky, Proust and Shakespeare, about what human beings are like and how we should lead our lives? It should also be noted that Girard does not show much interest in literature as a whole, only in a particular 'canon' of texts – consisting, as it happens, of writers who are concerned with the same themes as he is!

> The writers who interest me are obsessed with conflict as a subtle destroyer of the differential meaning it seems to inflate. I must share somewhat in that obsession . . . not literature as such, I believe, but certain literary texts are vital to my whole 'enterprise' as a researcher, much more vital than contemporary theory. Mine is a very selfish and pragmatic use of literary texts. If they cannot serve me, I leave them alone.
>
> (Girard, 1978, p. 224)

This formula: 'conflict as a subtle destroyer of the differential meaning it seems to inflate' is not an easy one to understand, but it is worth dwelling upon. Put very simply, Girard keeps returning to the paradox that the more the rivals in a conflict try to establish a difference between each other (by increasingly hostile gestures, for example), the more they in fact imitate one another, therefore becoming identical and even indistinguishable. This is evident in long-standing conflicts, such as the Troubles in Northern Ireland, which at their most intense were plagued by 'tit for tat' killings: one side carries out an execution, the other side repeats the action, and so on. Actions intended to establish difference have just the opposite effect: despite the frenzy of violence, it can look to the outsider as if the two sides are just mirror-images of each other (though obviously the participants themselves would take a very different view).

This chapter seeks to build on the preceding discussion of mimetic desire, by setting out a particular understanding of the nature of conflict, understood as 'a subtle destroyer of the differential meaning it seeks to inflate'. Desire is linked to conflict because it is mimetic. The second phase of Girard's theory seeks to investigate what happens when the rivalry which has been initiated because two parties share the same desire becomes more intense, and also becomes more widespread.

This involves developing Girard's theory in two ways. First, it means expanding the understanding of mimesis, from an account of interactions between two or a few agents to a more general explanation of social relations. Secondly, while up to now we have been looking with Girard at the modern period, through the lens of important novelists and playwrights, we now move into speculation upon the origins and nature of primitive or pre-state societies, that is, societies where institutions such as political and penal systems have not yet come into being.

The second phase of mimetic theory, therefore, has more to do with cultural anthropology rather than literature. It coincides with the publication of Girard's second book, *Violence and the Sacred* (French original 1972), a work which had an enormous impact and first brought Girard to widespread public attention, because of the startling claims it makes as to the interconnection between religion and cultural and social formation.

Girard's argument in this book can be summed up in a single, disturbing slogan: 'Violence is the heart and secret soul of the sacred.'

The line of Girard's argument in this text can be discerned in the distinction made in the last chapter, between two forms of mimetic desire: 'acquisitive' and 'metaphysical'. Serious conflicts may well begin with mimetic rivalry over an object which both parties want to acquire, yet they will seldom stay at this level. As the rivalry intensifies, the object will become less important, and the rivals become locked into a fascination with each other in a battle for prestige or 'recognition' (Hegel). This has more to do with one's very existence rather than any particular object. A very striking example of this can be found in Shakespeare's *Troilus and Cressida*, which, along with *A Midsummer Night's Dream*, is Girard's 'bible' for understanding mimetic desire. This bitterly satirical play centres on the action of the Trojan War, which, according to Shakespeare, is far from being the heroic conflict portrayed in Homer's epic poetry. Just the opposite – it is literally a pointless contest fought out by arrogant, stupid men. The Greeks are fighting to win back Helen because the Trojans abducted her. The Trojans insist on hanging onto Helen because the Greeks want her. Meanwhile, as time goes by, Helen's beauty fades a little more, and the justification for fighting over her becomes weaker. Each day the soldiers march onto the battlefield to win the military prowess which has now become an end in itself. They resemble an art dealer who has paid millions of pounds for a painting, and is therefore psychologically incapable of admitting that it just might be a forgery. This is the point made by Troilus when he observes bitterly: 'Fools on both sides! Helen must needs be fair/When with your blood you daily paint her thus.' Not for the last time in history, a young soldier asks: 'What are we fighting for?'

It is important to notice that this second stage – from a conflict which is centred on an object, to one which is more to do with the relationship between the rivals as such – is still being governed according to mimetic interaction, as the participants imitate one another's hostile gestures. The term Girard uses is *reciprocity*. Just as a good reciprocal gesture might defuse a conflict (for example, if one rival offers the hand of friendship), so an expression of hostility or bad reciprocity by one of the parties will be imitated and probably amplified by the other, thus causing the antagonism to escalate. Girard is keen to stress that violence is a relationship: while we may more readily think of the kind of anonymous violence that muggers inflict on their victims in inner cities, in fact many acts of violence take place between people who have known each other, and perhaps who have lived closely with one another, for a long period of time. How is it that close relationships like this can change so drastically and often suddenly? Precisely, says Girard, because such relationships are inherently unstable, built as they are upon the shifting foundations of mimetic desire.

The example of the Greeks and Trojans, and indeed of more

recent conflicts which seem to have little or no purpose to them, remind us that Girard's theory is an attempt to explain human relations on a broad social scale, and not just between two or three individuals. We have seen in the last chapter that it relates in particular to aspects of society in the modern period, when social stratification is gradually eroded, and hierarchical safeguards which were in place to channel and control mimetic unrest become less effective. The process which Girard traced in his novelists, from external (safe) mediation to internal (dangerous) mediation – from tall to squat triangles, if you will – is in fact the process of modernity itself, as it unfolds into the democratic era, the age of *ressentiment*.

The most important thinker with regard to this development is Thomas Hobbes (1588–1679), the father of modern political philosophy. While Hobbes' analysis of human nature in *Leviathan* (1651) coincides a great deal with mimetic theory, there is a crucial divergence between Girard and Hobbes when it comes to describing how communities deal with the problems generated by mimetic competition. First, let us look again at Hobbes and see the similarities. As we have seen, in Chapter 13 of *Leviathan*, he acknowledges the problem of competition among men of equal social status:

> For every man looketh that his companion should value him, at the same rate he sets upon himselfe . . . so that in the nature of man, we find three principall causes of quarrell. First, Competition; Secondly, Diffidence; Thirdly, Glory.

As we have noted, 'diffidence' here does not mean humility, rather it is the wariness which people show towards each other, precisely because they are of roughly equal ability, with no one noticeably stronger than the others. This diffidence is at the same time a source of self-assertion, since each desires the esteem or 'recognition' of the others. As Hobbes famously notes in the same chapter, such a state of unease can only be adequately described as a permanent and pervasive state of war:

> Hereby it is manifest, that during the time men live without a common Power to keep them all in awe, they are in that condition which is called Warre; and such a warre, as is of every man, against every man. For WARRE

consisteth not in Battell onely, or the act of fighting; but in a tract of time, wherein the Will to contend by Battell is sufficiently known . . . so the nature of War, consisteth not in actuall fighting; but in the known disposition thereto, during all the time there is no assurance to the contrary. All other time is PEACE. Whatsoever therefore is consequent to a time of Warre, where every man is Enemy to every man; the same is consequent to the time, wherein men live without other security, than what their own strength, and their own invention shall furnish them withall. In such condition, there is no place for Industry; because the fruit thereof is uncertain: and consequently no Culture of the Earth; no Navigation, nor use of the commodities that may be imported by Sea; no commodious Building; no Instruments of moving, and removing such things as require much force; no Knowledge of the face of the Earth; no account of Time; no Arts; no Letters; no Society; and which is worst of all, continuall feare, and danger of violent death; And the life of man, solitary, poore, nasty, brutish, and short.

It is the kind of bleak landscape we are familiar with from post-nuclear apocalypse literature and films, such as *Mad Max*. In fact, the actual political background to *Leviathan* is stark enough: the Civil War in England and, more importantly, the Thirty Years' War, which devastated Europe from 1618 to 1648. What Hobbes is saying is that this kind of nightmarish social meltdown, far from being exceptional in human affairs, should actually be recognised as the 'natural' state of human coexistence, before the emergence of social and political institutions which contain and control the human propensity for conflict. By imagining this scenario of 'the state of nature' and the 'war of all against all' which it entails, Hobbes sets out what he sees as the function and origins of political institutions, above all the monarchy. He offers both a description of the genesis of absolute sovereignty, and a justification of it. For Hobbes, the problem of universal strife is solved when all factions and parties simultaneously surrender their military strength and capability into the hands of one supreme and sovereign authority, one who therefore has a monopoly of the means of violence.

A modern parable, well known to most English schoolboys, which illustrates this state of affairs, would be William Golding's 1959 novel *Lord of the Flies*. A group of schoolboys, stranded on an island with no parental control, revert to a state of murderous nature, until order is restored at the end by the arrival of a naval ship. The function of the sovereign in Hobbes, and of the naval officer, dressed in immaculate whites, who appears at the end of Golding's novel, has in fact religious overtones, which are summed up in the Greek term *katéchon*. This word appears, rather mysteriously, in the New Testament (1 Thessalonians), meaning a 'restraining force'. It seems to refer to the divine power, holding back the forces of chaos and destruction which will be unleashed at the end of time. More generally, the *katéchon* introduces us to a conception of politics where the overriding purpose of political institutions is the restraint of conflict. This is the kind of thing the Roman Empire excelled at, imposing its *pax Romana* on other peoples by virtue of its military superiority. (In the same way, the United States in the present day, when it chooses to behave as a 'global policeman', takes on the function of a *katéchon*.) This is an essentially pessimistic view of human affairs, since it assumes that peaceful coexistence is impossible for human beings unless some superior force guarantees it coercively. Of course, proponents of the *katéchon* approach would respond that this is not pessimism but realism.

So, for Hobbes, social stability is achieved when people realise their need of a *katéchon*, that is, a sovereign, an all-powerful restraining force whose authority all members of the group agree to recognise, for the sake of their common safety and well-being. He names this force after the biblical monster, Leviathan. Girard's fundamental opposition to this kind of explanation is nothing to do with its pessimism or conservatism: he simply thinks the scenario set out by Hobbes (and by other social contract theorists) is highly implausible. Girard is scornful of the idea that a group of people who are at each others' throats would have the capacity, *precisely at the moment when the conflict is at its most intense*, to cease hostilities and recognise that they need to work out a social contract. This calm, rational approach to the problem betrays a lack of imagination as to how impassioned and enraged groups actually behave. Girard jests here about Hobbes' Englishness, and imagines the 'war of all against all' concluding with people sitting down and sorting out their differences over a nice cup of tea. He accepts Hobbes' scenario of a universal strife, but cannot go along with Hobbes' description of how this crisis comes to be resolved.

Girard offers what he regards as a more satisfactory and plausible explanation of how societies establish or regain a harmonious equilibrium, but to understand this requires a closer look at the nature of the crisis under discussion. We have noted the phenomenon of 'internal mediation', that is, in a context where individuals are in close proximity with one another's desires, and where the social barriers which would prevent mimetic rivalry from developing have been eroded. In the modern era there are institutions such as police, armies, judiciary, which ensure for the most part that violence does not get out of hand. But what happens in contexts where these institutions are not in place, either because they have broken down, or because they have not yet come into existence?

Here, the action of metaphysical desire can be very dangerous indeed, and may be likened to a contagious disease. Violence 'spreads', like an epidemic or a wildfire; we recall that there are no strong instinctual brakes on human aggression. Girard suggests indeed that symbols such as the plague, fire, flood, and so on, when these appear in myths and legends, are veiled references to an escalating mimetic crisis. In primitive social contexts, where no clear distinction exists between the social and natural orders, such symbols are especially appropriate. Girard points to a number of examples from literature and mythology where this link between pestilence and a society in meltdown can be discerned: for example, in the Prologue to *Oedipus Rex*, where the priest describes to Oedipus a famine which threatens to wipe out the city of Thebes; or in the ten plagues which smite the Egyptians in Exodus, where Girard sees the element of rivalry in the struggle between Moses and the Egyptian sorcerers.

At the root of the crisis is the destruction of social differentiation, which can only lead to mimetic violence, as indicated by the important speech of Ulysses in *Troilus and Cressida* (I. 3. 75–133). In this play, a severe crisis of authority, or 'crisis of degree', has broken out in the camp of the Greek army. Achilles, the hero and champion of the Greeks, openly flouts the leadership of Agamemnon, and as a result a spirit of destructive rivalry is now rife throughout the camp.

Ulysses' speech is a superb diagnosis and description of the mimetic crisis which arises from a 'neglection of degree', and is worth quoting at length:

> O! When degree is shak'd,
> Which is the ladder to all high designs,
> The enterprise is sick. How could communities,
> Degrees in schools, and brotherhoods in cities,
> Peaceful commerce from dividable shores,
> The primogenitive and due of birth,
> Prerogative of age, crowns, sceptres, laurels,
> But by degree, stand in authentic place?
> Take but degree away, untune that string,
> And, hark! what discord follows; each thing meets
> In mere oppugnancy: the bounded waters
> Should lift their bosoms higher than the shores,
> And make a sop of all this solid globe:
> Strength should be lord of imbecility
> And the rude son should strike his father dead:
> Force should be right; or rather right and wrong –
> Between whose endless jar justice resides –
> Should lose their names, and so should justice too.
> Then every thing includes itself in power,
> Power into will, will into appetite;
> And appetite, a universal wolf,
> So doubly seconded with will and power,
> Must make perforce a universal prey,
> And last eat up himself.
>
> (I. 3. 101–124)

The predatory imagery at the end is appropriate, since one of the distorting effects of violence is to make the combatants seem 'monstrous' to one another. This is the extreme case of undifferentiation, because a 'monster' is a creature in which human and animal qualities are mixed. As we are only too aware, in a prolonged conflict each side can lose sight of the humanity of the other. Either the enemy are regarded as less than human, therefore 'bestial', or they are regarded as supremely evil, and 'demonised'. There is a hallucinatory effect at work, which Girard relates once again to many manifestations of the 'monstrous' in myth and literature; a society in mimetic crisis has difficulty in holding on even to the most basic of classifications, such as human or non-human.

Once again, Shakespeare provides rich examples. As we have seen, in *A Theatre of Envy* Girard has six essays on *A Midsummer Night's Dream,* which he regards as a very precise record of the mechanics of mimetic desire and the ensuing crisis. The 'translations' and distortions which take place on this midsummer night, the dreamlike state which envelops the action and the characters, the animal imagery which is quickly interchanged with metaphors of divine adoration as the young lovers repeatedly switch their allegiances – all testify to the ferocity of the mimetic crisis and give the lie to the belief of the lovers that their desires are autonomous and stable.

This is crucially important. We are used to thinking that conflict arises from difference – different religions, tribes or nations at loggerheads with one another – but in fact Girard here insists that it is the *erosion* of differences which is the dangerous trigger for violence. It is the fear of sameness, the loss of distinguishing characteristics, which catalyses conflict (the very opposite of what a certain famous but annoyingly banal song by John Lennon would have us imagine). We are back with a graphic description of Hobbes' 'war of all against all', and with the question, once again: how does an ordered and harmonious society emerge from this crisis, and not simply find itself engulfed in frenzied self-destruction? The question is even more acute if we agree with Girard that 'social contract' theories at this point are unsatisfactory.

Girard's explanation is tidier, because the dynamic of mimesis itself provides the solution to the mimetic crisis, so he does not have to introduce new factors external to the situation. Just as acquisitive mimesis started the escalation of conflict, so mimesis in the opposite direction can end it. This new mimesis comes about because the original object of envy has now disappeared from view. In place of this original object of contention we now have the direct conflict of the opponents: metaphysical mimesis. Because the object is no longer central, a new basis for unity can be found. The violence against one of the contestants can be imitated by others without necessarily breeding new rivalry – on the contrary, imitating a violent action against a combatant will lead to reconciliation. A pointing finger, a chance blow, a slight curse against him or her will be repeated by others, and quickly the strife of 'all against all' becomes a war of (nearly) all against one, or some. The victim will be set upon by the whole group; he or she may be expelled, or put to death.

This new mimesis of 'all against one' unites rather than divides. It is the reconciliation and sense of unity of the lynch mob, as all the violence and hate that they previously directed at one another are now vented upon a single victim. This victim is the embodiment of all evil, and appears to the mob to be responsible for the crisis. He or she is well known to all of us in our classrooms and playgrounds, our workplaces, our families and even our church communities. Girard gives this victim its everyday name, 'scapegoat', while he calls this process, by which the mimetic crisis is resolved, the 'scapegoat mechanism'.

Girard is using the term precisely in its everyday sense, and not with reference to the 'scapegoat' mentioned in Leviticus 16. This last is a conscious religious rite, in which the high priest transfers, by the laying on of hands, the sins of the people onto a goat, who is then cast out into the wilderness. Girard is not concerned with this conscious ritual, but with the more popular meaning of 'scapegoating' as a spontaneous and unconscious psychological mechanism, by which someone is falsely accused and victimised. Needless to say, although there is a degree of randomness as to who gets singled out as the scapegoat, it transpires that the person or group is usually chosen because they are especially vulnerable or marginal to begin with. The 'outsider' or stranger is a strong candidate, because he or she is less likely to have family or friends who can come to their defence (Oedipus would be a striking example of this). By the same token, many of the victims of witch-hunts during the medieval period happened to be single women living on their own. The potential victim may also be singled out because he or she is physically or mentally abnormal or defective in some way (Oedipus has a limp). We never learn the name of the boy who is persecuted and falls to his death in *Lord of the Flies*: the other boys simply call him 'Piggy' – he is overweight, asthmatic and wears glasses.

A community deals with its violence by channelling it. In this sense the solution to the threat of outright violence contains violence, in the two senses of 'contains': it involves controlled, limited use of violence, in order to prevent a much more widespread violence from engulfing and destroying the whole group. In fact there are two ways in which the violence can be channelled away from the community at large. We have mentioned one, the scapegoat mechanism, which sees the violence heaped on an 'enemy within'. But the violence can also be channelled outwards, towards an external enemy. This is succinctly conveyed by Aeschylus in *The Eumenides*, when the Chorus articulates the true nature of political unity: a sentiment of common feeling, on the one hand, and of hatred directed towards an external enemy on the other. This is the 'pledge of common hate and common friendship'.

> Nevermore these walls within
> Shall echo fierce sedition's din,
> Unslaked with blood and crime;
> The thirsty dust shall nevermore
> Suck up the darkly streaming gore
> Of civic broils, shed out in wrath
> And vengeance, crying death for death!
> But man with man and state with state
> Shall vow the pledge of common hate
> And common friendship, that for man
> Hath oft made blessing, out of ban,
> Be ours unto all time.
>   (*Eumenides*, 978–87)

Both types of violence are explored by Shakespeare. *Julius Caesar* is a point-by-point exposition of the different stages of the 'crisis of degree', from the first mutterings of conspiracy to the act of Caesar's murder. The factional rivalry between Caesar and other prominent Romans is threatening civil disintegration, though gradually the problem is perceived as one of Caesar alone gaining too much power. He emerges as the necessary victim who must die, and yet whose blood will revivify Rome. The speech of Brutus, in which the conspirators are exhorted to be 'sacrificers' not 'butchers', captures exactly the ambivalence towards the sacred victim (as we shall see, Girard calls this ambiguity a 'double transference'). In short, the play as a whole marvellously exemplifies the entire scapegoating process.

In another Shakespeare play, the second example of unifying violence mentioned in the *Eumenides* – that is, violence which is turned outwards against a common enemy – is set out in astonishing conciseness. The speaker here is King Henry IV, who is exhausted with putting down the rebellions which have afflicted his reign, and longs only to unite the forces which have been so bitterly divided in 'civil butchery' into a single military project. What is the project? A Crusade, no less, to liberate the holy fields, once walked by those same blessed feet which were nailed on the cross 'for our advantage':

> So shaken as we are, so wan with care,
> Find we a time for frighted peace to pant,
> And breathe short-winded accents of new broils
> To be commenc'd in strands afar remote.
> No more the thirsty entrance of this soil
> Shall daub her lips with her own children's blood;
> No more shall trenching war channel her fields,
> Nor bruise her flowerets with the armed hoofs
> Of hostile paces: those opposed eyes,
> Which like the meteors of a troubled heaven,
> All of one nature, of one substance bred,
> Did lately meet in the intestine shock
> And furious close of civil butchery,
> Shall now, in mutual well-beseeming ranks,
> March all one way, and be no more oppos'd
> Against acquaintance, kindred and allies:
> The edge of war, like an ill-sheathed knife,
> No more shall cut his master. Therefore, friends,
> As far as to the sepulchre of Christ, –
> Whose soldier now, under whose blessed cross
> We are impressed and engag'd to fight, –
> Forthwith a power of English shall we levy,
> Whose arms were moulded in their mother's womb
> To chase these pagans in those holy fields
> Over whose acres walk'd those blessed feet
> Which fourteen hundred years ago were nail'd
> For our advantage on the bitter cross.
>
> (*Henry IV Part I*: I. 1. 1–27)

The insight held up here by Aeschylus and Shakespeare is familiar to every political leader wishing to reinforce his or her popularity. If the people are to remain united, they need a common enemy, within or without. The scapegoating process will take care of the enemy within. If the enemy is to be an external one, then starting a war – the holier the better – is the trusted way forward.

The religious language and imagery of these passages are not accidental. Both types of unifying violence are a kind of 'holy war'. In the scapegoat mechanism, everything negative is loaded upon the victim. But because the victim has brought about the reconciliation of the community, he or she also comes to be credited with positive features. Girard describes this paradoxical effect as a 'double transference'. That is, as well as a transference of aggressivity by the persecutors onto the victim, there is also a transference of reconciliation, as the victim is associated with the catharsis that has come about. Previously, the persecutors lost their bearings in the hallucinatory world of 'monstrous doubles'; now they can only see their victim in terms of the double transference.

Far from recognising and accepting their responsibility for the crisis and their escape from it, both effects – one good, the other evil – are attributed by the persecutors to the victim, who is now himself both absolutely good and absolutely evil. All the 'monstrosity' of the crisis is incarnated in a single person. Girard explains this by drawing on Rudolf Otto's analysis of 'the Holy' as a meeting together of the '*fascinosum*' and '*tremendum*'. In short, the persecutors come to conceive of their victim as a god, or at least as having an exalted transcendent status, and from now on they hold themselves under his sway.

> . . . [O]ne must postulate a mimetic crisis of such duration and severity that the sudden resolution, at the expense of a single victim, has the effect of a miraculous deliverance. The experience of a supremely evil and then beneficient being, whose appearance and disappearance are punctuated by collective murder, cannot fail to be literally *gripping*. The community that was once so terribly stricken suddenly finds itself free of antagonism, completely delivered. It is therefore comprehensible that such a community would be henceforth wholly animated by a desire for peace, and bent on preserving the miraculous calm apparently granted to it by the fearful and benign being that had somehow descended upon it. The community

will thus direct all future action under the sign of that being, as if carrying out the instructions it had left. In summary, the community attempts to consolidate its fragile hold on things under the still strong impressions of the crisis and its resolution, believing itself to be under the guidance of the victim itself.

(Girard, 1987a, p. 28)

Religious awe has its origin in the act of scapegoating. Such religion has nothing to do with a genuinely transcendent God, distinct from the human world, rather it is a phenomenon created unconsciously by humans themselves. For the persecutors, it simply appears that a transcendent external power is at work. Newly reconciled by their violence, they feel themselves to be taken up in a religious process. The origin of religion, therefore, is to be found in 'sacrifice', which is none other than the violent extermination of the scapegoat.

This extraordinary claim should be set in the context of a wider and even more extraordinary one. The kind of experience Girard is describing is so impressive, that it is not inconceivable that the most basic kinds of cultural institutions are founded upon an event of this nature. One aspect of religion is the establishment of the distinction between 'sacred' and profane'; here, it is God (in the form of the victim) who is sacred, the society is profane. What about other fundamental differences, such as time and space? The event of sacrifice can be said to divide time into a before (the time of crisis) and after (the time of reconciliation). There is also an 'inside' and an 'outside', once again the community and the expelled victim respectively. Palaver (2003, pp. 226–9) cites a wide range of indicators as to the ordering function of the scapegoat mechanism on a social and cultural, as well as religious, level: Cain as the biblical founder of cities; the origins of stratified society according to Hindu mythology; Heraclitus' fragment about 'Strife being the father and king of all things'. Girard himself, following Durkheim and Eliade, points to the importance of sacred locations such as tombs, the hearth, etc., forming the centre of the community; symbolic sites of unification which gave birth to religious forms and to the establishment of spatial and temporal relationships. And he also points to the evidence which links these sites with surrogate victimhood.

This intuition of an intimate connection between human culture and sacrificial violence, particularly a foundational violence or sacrifice (the German word is *Bauopfer*) has been explored by Walter Burkert as a practice behind which lies the conviction that 'a house, a bridge, a dam, will only be secure if a corpse lies underneath it' (Burkert, 1983). The theme of the *Bauopfer* is a constant in myth and literature, e.g. in the story of the murder of Remus, which is at the same time the founding of the city of Rome. In the Bible, the fratricide Cain is also the founder of urban culture and civilisation – once again, a suggested link between murder and foundations. The theme is well conveyed by W. H. Auden, in his poem 'Vespers', which describes a meeting between the speaker, who is a romantic idealist, and a political radical; that is, between an 'Arcadian' and a 'Utopian':

> Was it (as it must look to any god of cross-roads) simply a
>   fortuitous intersection of life-paths, loyalty to different fibs?
> Or also a rendez-vous between two accomplices who, in spite
>   of themselves, cannot resist meeting
> to remind the other (do both, at bottom, desire truth?) of that
>   half of their secret which he would most like to forget,
> forcing us both, for a fraction of a second, to remember our
>   victim (but for him I could forget the blood, but for me he
>   could forget the innocence),
> on whose immolation (call him Abel, Remus, whom you
>   will, it is one Sin Offering) arcadias, utopias, our dear old
>   bag of a democracy are alike founded:
> For without a cement of blood (it must be human, it must be
>   innocent) no secular wall can safely stand.
>
>   'Vespers' from *Horae Canonicae*

Girard's next step is to indicate how the central elements of all religions are related to the victimage mechanism. Three of these are especially important: *myths*, *rites*, and *taboos or prohibitions*. Myths tell the story of the persecution from the perspective of the victor, the lyncher; rites are the controlled repetition of the sacrificial action, through which the community gains renewed strength and unanimity, especially where these rites involve sacrifices (victims); taboos and prohibitions are in place so that there will be no repetition of the rivalry which might lead to a new crisis.

It should be noted that Girard's treatment of prohibitions and ritual has a particularly elegant twist here, since he is offering a plausible explanation for two phenomena which appear to be opposed to one another. Prohibitions or taboos 'cordon off' the object of potential rivalry, whether this be women, food, or other possessions of the group leader, so that differentiation and hierarchy within a group are preserved, and conflict is avoided. Many rituals seem to do the exact opposite: they involve a relaxation of prohibitions, so that hierarchical distinctions are reversed or temporally abolished, and actions which are normally banned may be carried out in a ritualised setting (for example, ritual incest). The sacrificial rite itself is to be understood as a re-enactment of the violent scapegoating. We make sense of this, says Girard, if we recognise that both prohibitions and rites are intended to avert the crisis of mimetic conflict, only they do so in different ways and at different stages of the conflict. Whereas prohibitions would be a normal way of doing this when social conditions are relatively stable, in cases where the mimetic pressure is more extreme a more radical solution is required; namely a controlled, 'safe' re-enactment of the crisis itself. This works in the same way that a small dose of poison or virus may be used as an antidote to the poison itself in its more dangerous form.

In the light of these insights, an account from a 2001 newspaper article by Rahul Bedi requires no further commentary. The article is headlined: 'Priest takes murdered king's soul into exile':

> A Nepali priest rode off on an elephant for a lifetime of exile yesterday in a ceremony designed to exorcise the ghosts of the royal family massacre. Wearing the late King Birendra's shoes, socks and spectacles, Durga Prasad Sapkota was deemed by Nepalese Hindu ritual to be taking the king's spirit with him to a remote mountainous region where he will spend the rest of his life as an 'unholy outcast'. Devout Nepalis believe his departure will ease the troubles in the country since the massacre on June 1, when Crown Prince Dipendra murdered nine members of the royal family before fatally shooting himself. Before leaving Kathmandu, the frail 75-year-old Brahmin, who volunteered for the role, sat in a tent on the banks of the Bagmati river and ate 84 different items, including rice and vegetables, from silver bowls. In ancient

times, he would have eaten part of the king's brain, but yesterday the leg of a sacrificed goat served the purpose. A silver crown with a long white plume, similar to the king's, was placed on Sapkota's head and he sat under a bamboo canopy, signifying the throne. Prime Minister Girija Prasad Koirala then offered the priest money before asking him if he was happy. 'I am happy, I have everything now. I just don't have a house. I need a house,' replied Sapkota. According to tradition, the banished priest is granted all his demands. He was, however, given £8,000 raised from an appeal before mounting the brightly painted elephant that will remain with him in exile.

Violence and the Sacred: A Closer Look

The thesis put forward in *La Violence et le sacré* is, to put it mildly, quite a lot to take in. It is easy to understand why the book had such a considerable impact when it came out in 1972. I will expand this summary of Girard's theory with the help of Burton Mack's introduction of mimetic theory in *Violent Origins* (1987). This book is a record of Girard's engagement with two other theorists (Walter Burkert and Jonathan Z. Smith), one of whom offers a similarly grand explanatory account of religion. The conference itself was initiated by Burton Mack, and that section of his introductory essay which relates to Girard (pp. 6–22) is a careful and lucid attempt to reconstruct Girard's intellectual journey; though it should be acknowledged that in general Mack expresses a strong resistance to Girard's view of the New Testament writings as anti-persecution texts (Mack, 1985).

Burton Mack specifies the central problem which emerges at this point in René Girard's astonishing theory. According to Girard, mimetic desire is not recognised by individuals on an everyday basis, and at the level of cultural institutions the mythical mentality holds sway, so that the horrible truth of the victimage killing is concealed:

> So where do we look to see the enactment according to the original script? The data appear not to be available. Cultural artefacts are structured so as to hide the mechanisms of violence, and the mechanisms are designed so as to conceal even themselves. A disclosure is required, but

what veil can be lifted? How, in fact, has Girard himself made the discovery?

(Mack, 1987, p. 11)

The discovery is made, as we have seen in the previous chapter, in the course of Girard's reading of literature. 'Girard moves easily from culture to culture, epoch to epoch, text to text, novel to myth, with a single assumption about language and a single method for its critical reading ... he is a literary critic who has dared to propose a theory of religion on the basis of his criticism.' And yet it is only in Chapter 6 of *Violence and the Sacred*, and then only in a footnote, that we find reference to *Deceit, Desire and the Novel*. Mack asks where the notion of mimetic desire has come from, though he traces its inspiration in Girard not to Hegel, but to a tradition of reflection in French thought which takes in Rousseau, Durkheim, Sartre and others.

As Mack points out, Chapter 6 of *Violence and the Sacred* ('From Mimetic Desire to the Monstrous Double') is the one on which the argument of the whole book hinges; here, Girard grounds his theory of the victimage mechanism. Before this, we have an examination of the ancient texts which exemplify the mechanism (for example, myths of Oedipus and Dionysus), while the chapters which follow deal with Freud and Lévi-Strauss, in order that Girard's hypothesis may be set in context. It is from Chapter 6 that we may work out how Girard moved from mimetic desire, as set out in his book on the novel, to the theory of sacrificial violence. Mack conjectures that it is Girard's reading of *The Bacchae* by Euripedes which provides the bridge between the two phases, since in this play the two themes – mimetic contagion and sacrificial violence – are both present. 'Texts are in touch with the mechanisms and events that generate social structures and their history.' With this play, the doors are opened for Girard to read the rich archive of texts in the history of religion, and his theory expands in scope accordingly.

> By combining the two literatures (novels with mimetic plots and myths of killing), Girard produces the full dramatic sequence. Each needs the other as its comple-ment. Taken together, literature and myth show that mimetic rivalry leads to the monstrous double and the killing, and that it does so in such a way as to effect their

erasure in the subsequent reflection on the event. Euripedes' dramatic text is important because it shows this relationship between literature and myth ... myths are the texts most proximate to the crucial, climactic event of the drama, but without great literature to interpret them and expose what they conceal, we never would have known this.

(Mack, 1987, p. 17)

From this, we have a threefold ranking of text-types: myths, (great) literature, and criticism. Myths are closest to the rationalisations that occur in primitive religions, but for that reason can only reinforce their concealment of violence. Great literature, by contrast (meaning Greek tragedies, Shakespeare, the major novelists), is able to disclose aspects of the mechanism that myth conceals. But it is the task of the critic to 'expose the mechanism for what it is – namely, the generative matrix of social existence'. From this, as Girard indicates in the closing chapters of *Violence and the Sacred*, a theory of history emerges, summarised thus by Mack:

Myth is most appropriate to the primitive forms of religion and society; literature occurs in societies that find it possible to develop legal systems to serve the religious function; and the kind of criticism Girard calls for is most appropriate for our own time when what he calls the 'sacrificial crisis' has belatedly emerged even with the societies of law.

(Mack, p. 21)

Girard and Freud

Two chapters in *Violence and the Sacred* deal with aspects of Sigmund Freud's work: Chapter 7, 'Freud and the Oedipus Complex' and Chapter 8, '*Totem and Taboo* and the Incest Problem'. Girard's third major work, *Things Hidden Since the Foundation of the World*, contains a long section on 'Interdividual Psychology', which is an engagement with Freud's theories of narcissism and, again, the Oedipus complex. As Mack points out, in *Violence and the Sacred* Girard 'all but tells us that Freud was his model, and that he achieved his theory of mimetic desire in the struggle to understand Freud'. Whatever similarities may appear between the hypothesis of the

Oedipus complex and that of mimetic desire, the big difference that emerges between them is that for Girard desire is more 'free-floating' than for Freud. The model/rival does not have to be the father, nor is the object of desire necessarily the mother; neither model nor object are predetermined. If this is accepted, mimetic theory is able to account for psycho-social dynamics much more elegantly, and without some of the entanglements that bedevilled Freud as he struggled to hang on to the Oedipal configuration. Mack suggests that Girard's thinking is more nourished at this point by contemporary French theorists such as Lacan, who seek to use psychoanalytical theory to ground a theory of social formation which does not rely on the Oedipal hypothesis.

The theme is a large one, and does get very technical, though some of the contradictions are clearly illustrated in Girard's response to Freud's 1913 work, *Totem and Taboo*. There are striking similarities between Freud's account of a founding murder and Girard's, and for this reason Girard feels the text should have received more attention than it has done. Freud argues that the taboo of incest originates in the envy of the primal tribe towards their father, concerning the women cordoned off for his own use. The sons murder the father, but then commemorate the killing ritually and repeat the sexual prohibition, out of fear and guilt towards the dead leader. Girard acknowledges from the start that this text has been almost universally rejected by critics, principally because of its circular argumentation regarding the sexual monopoly of the dominant male, and subsequent prohibitions concerning incest. He is unwilling to write off the text too quickly, however, and in any event, if this is a case of Freud going seriously astray, that in itself is worth investigating. In one important passage in *Totem and Taboo*, Freud discusses the nature and meaning of tragedy, and in particular of the mysterious 'tragic guilt' which attaches itself to the Hero:

> But why had the Hero of tragedy to suffer? And what was the meaning of this 'tragic guilt'? I will cut the discussion short and give a quick reply. He had to suffer because he was the primal father, the Hero of the great primeval tragedy which was being re-enacted with a tendentious twist; and the tragic guilt was the guilt which he had to take on himself in order to relieve the Chorus from theirs.

> The scene upon the stage was derived from the historical scene through a process of systematic distortion – one might even say, as the product of a refined hypocrisy . . . The crime which was thrown on to his shoulders, presumptuousness and rebelliousness against a great authority, was precisely the crime for which the members of the Chorus, the company of brothers, were responsible. Thus the tragic Hero became, though it might be against his will, the redeemer of the Chorus.
>
> (*Totem and Taboo*, pp. 155–6)

It is hard not to be impressed by the similarities with Girard's own theory of the surrogate victim. For both Girard and Freud, 'tragedy is thus defined as a tendentious re-enactment, a mythic inversion of an event that actually took place' but which is thereafter subject to a process of 'systematic distortion'. Girard immediately states, however, the differences between them. Principal among these is that Freud speaks of a single murder, that of an actual father, which took place at a single moment. This father was an oppressive monster during his life, but is transformed at death into a hero figure. By contrast, mimetic theory is not committed to a single victim, the father; therefore it can assert that sacrificial killings are repeated over a long period of time.

What is astonishing is that in the course of his discussion of tragedy, Freud makes not a single reference to *Oedipus the King*, though he cites other tragedies, and even though this tragedy of father-murder would fit perfectly the argument he is trying to construct. Throughout *Totem and Taboo* Oedipus is conspicuous by his absence – though for Girard this is a conscious move on Freud's part, rather than a classic case of a Freudian 'slip'. The simple explanation is that the theory of the actual father-murder which Freud puts forward here is incompatible with the official psychoanalytical version of the Oedipus complex. On this latter version, the unconscious desires are by definition *not* carried to fulfilment; so the tragedy of *Oedipus the King* cannot simultaneously be put forward as a demonstration of two incompatible situations. Freud recognises this, and sidesteps the issue by not mentioning Oedipus at all. In so doing, says Girard, he also steps away from a line of enquiry that would possibly be more fruitful than either Oedipus as repressed desire or Oedipus as actual parricide: the question of the surrogate victim. What hinders Freud, here and elsewhere, is his strong protectiveness towards the theory of psychoanalysis, and the Oedipus complex in particular.

Freud is nearer the mark when he suggests another reason (other than guilt) as to why the sons maintain their ban on the prohibited women, even after the murder of the father who had previously blocked access to them. The reason is that they fear that they would become rivals, whose sexual desires would involve them in a struggle of all against all unless they agree to institute a law against incest. (Freud even acknowledges that 'sexual desires do not unite men, but divide them'.) The centre of attention, as it were, has shifted from the father to the enemy brothers. The kind of arrangement they have to come to would be necessary, even if the father had never existed. This, for Girard, is the heart of the matter, and when Freud is not blinkered by his psychoanalytical lens he is similarly alert to the important themes: undifferentiation, enemy brothers on the brink of a war against all.

Girard's insights, gleaned from reading between the lines of *Totem and Taboo*, are supported by his reading of *Moses and Monotheism*, in which the place of the murdered father is taken by Moses, put to death by the Israelites. This latter work operates with a large social framework (the Jewish nation, people, religion), which is a corrective, as it were, of the dominance of the family in *Totem and Taboo*. And it is precisely this latter dimension that obscures Freud's vision; he is fixated upon the family constellation and its sexuality. The weakness of *Totem and Taboo*, for Girard, is not the theme of collective murder, but the morass of psychoanalytical material that obscures it. Despite Freud's frequent appeals to what analysis has demonstrated or revealed, says Girard, 'in fact the father explains nothing. If we hope to get to the root of the matter we must put the father out of our minds . . .' What is significant for the community is not the identity of the victim, but his role as a unifying agent, or scapegoat, and this could in fact be any member of the group: 'The "murdered father" theory of *Totem and Taboo* is clearly indefensible, but the vulnerable element is not the "murder" but the "father"' (Girard, 1977, p. 216).

Girard's succinct judgement on Freud in these two works is as follows: only by introducing the theory of the surrogate victim into the fragmented and contradictory Freudian corpus does the jigsaw come together. 'We have only to cease regarding Freud's thought in terms of infallible dogma to see that he was always fundamentally concerned with the operation of the surrogate victim' (p. 217).

CHAPTER 3

Dionysus versus 'The Crucified'

CHAPTER SUMMARY

1. The scapegoating process enables a community in crisis to recover or preserve its equilibrium. This is only effective if the community is able to disguise from itself the true nature of what it is doing. None of the religious practices – myths, prohibitions and rituals – declares openly what is happening. René Girard understands 'myth' to mean the story which a community tells of its own origins – a story which merely hints at, but never openly reveals, the violence of these origins. In this sense 'myth' is derived from the same root as 'mute': myths perpetuate a silence about violent scapegoating. A parable by Kafka, *In the Penal Colony*, gives a horrific illustration of the violent sacred in operation, and in decline.

2. After *Violence and the Sacred* appears in 1972, it is several years before Girard feels ready to examine the Bible with the same attention as he has devoted to anthropological and non-Christian mythical texts. When he does so, he is convinced that the whole thrust of the biblical revelation runs in the opposite direction to myth as he has defined it, even though the Bible does contain mythical material. God is on the side of the innocent victim, not of the persecutors; the Bible operates as a critique and condemnation of sacrificial scapegoating, not as an example of it.

3. For this reason, Girard speaks of an opposition of 'myth' and 'gospel'; the Gospel is the biblical spirit which exposes the truth of violent origins, takes the side of the victim, and works towards the overcoming of scapegoating as a viable means of social formation. The distinction can in a sense be seen as similar to that between the 'Romantic Lie 'and 'novelistic truth', as these are discussed in Chapter 1. In each case, there is a struggle between two perspectives on human nature: one which denies the complicity of desire, religion and violence, the other which exposes it.

4. Girard cites numerous biblical passages in support of his theory, and a

selection of these is considered here: from the Old Testament, the Fall narrative in Genesis, the story of Abraham and Isaac, the Servant of Yahweh. In the New Testament, the teachings of Jesus, his prophetic critique of religion and above all the events of the Passion and Resurrection, all yield readings which are supportive of a mimetic interpretation: that Jesus' 'strategy' as the ambassador from a loving, non-violent Father is to expose and render ineffective the scapegoat process, so that the true God may be known.

5. The Passion of Jesus lends itself to a 'dramatic' interpretation, as Jesus allows a scapegoat crisis to be 'acted out', with himself at its centre. Like the Suffering Servant of Isaiah, however, his innocence, his refusal to seek for vengeance – and above all the vindication of God (who asserts Jesus' righteousness by raising him from the dead) combine to expose the truth of the persecution.

6. Girard's Christianity can appropriately be called 'Johannine'. He refers to the 'Logos' of John, meaning the truth of the Prologue to the Fourth Gospel, in which the Word comes into the world but is rejected by it. For John, the moment of Jesus' execution is also the moment of his exaltation. We are called to see the true face of God in the scapegoat, or Lamb of God, not the face of a persecuting deity.

7. Here also, the differences between Girard and Friedrich Nietzsche are made explicit. Girard is drawn to Nietzsche's insight about the unique significance of Christianity, and about the incompatibility of 'Dionysus' and 'the Crucified'. Nevertheless, Nietzsche sides with the 'life-affirming' values and ideology of Dionysus, which is why Girard, from the perspective of Christian revelation, describes his project as 'against – or anti – Nietzsche'.

As an introduction to the third, 'spectacular', phase of Girard's theory – the importance of the Gospel revelation as an unveiler of the scapegoat mechanism – I wish to consider a very disturbing short story by Franz Kafka, entitled *In the Penal Colony*. It tells of an explorer visiting an island prison colony, who is invited to watch the execution of an insubordinate prisoner. An officer and a soldier are in attendance. The officer shows off with grim relish the machine by which capital sentences have traditionally been carried out on the island: the condemned man, he explains, is strapped onto a bed with a battery attached. The bed vibrates in correspondence with 'the Harrow', a complicated array of quivering needles and spikes. When

these are set in motion, they 'write' in fine calligraphy the com-
mandment which the victim had transgressed, in this case the words
'HONOUR THY SUPERIORS'. The machine adorns this script
with elaborate flourishes across the entirety of the man's body, an
agonising process which takes place over a number of hours. During
this time, the officer explains enthusiastically, a significant transformation takes place in the victim:

> But how quiet he grows at just about the sixth hour!
> Enlightenment comes to the most dull-witted. It begins
> around the eyes. From there it radiates. A moment that
> might tempt one to get under the Harrow oneself.
> Nothing more happens than that the man begins to
> understand the inscription, he purses his mouth as if he
> were listening. You have seen how difficult it is to deci-
> pher the script with one's eyes; but our man deciphers it
> with his wounds. To be sure that is a hard task; he needs
> six hours to accomplish it, by that time the Harrow has
> pierced him quite through and casts him into the pit
> where he pitches down upon the blood and water and the
> cotton wool. Then the judgement has been fulfilled, and
> we, the soldier and I, bury him.

During this description, the officer anticipates – and dismisses – all
the liberal objections of the horrified explorer. He believes totally in
the justice and efficacy of this process and this apparatus. He is wor-
ried, however, that its days are numbered: the liberalism of the new
Commandant in charge of the colony, the difficulty of maintaining
the machine (it is beginning to creak, spare parts are hard to obtain),
the decline of the execution itself from a once dignified and popular public ritual to little more than a shabby ceremony, move him to
try and enlist the explorer's support, that as a visitor he might per-
suade the Commandant of the island of the value of this method of
ceremonial execution.

When the explorer finally explodes and announces his disgust at
the barbarism of the whole procedure, the officer falls silent. Then
he releases the prisoner, who all this time has been awaiting his fate.
He sets the machine to inscribe the words 'BE JUST', and he straps
himself onto the bed. Now the apparatus is put into motion, but it
quickly starts to go horribly wrong:

The Harrow was not writing, it was only jabbing, and the Bed was not turning the body over but only bringing it up quivering against the needles. The explorer wanted to do something, if possible, to bring the whole machine to a standstill, for this was no exquisite torture such as the officer desired, this was plain murder. He stretched out his hands, but at that moment the Harrow rose with the body spitted on it and moved to the side, as it usually did only when the twelfth hour had come. Blood was flowing in a hundred streams, not mingled with water, the water jets too had failed to function. And now the last action failed to fulfil itself, the body did not drop off the long needles, streaming with blood it went on hanging over the pit without falling into it. The Harrow tried to move back to its old position, but as if it had itself noticed that it had not yet got rid of its burden it stuck after all where it was, over the pit . . . And here, almost against his will, he had to look at the face of the corpse. It was as it had been in life; no sign was visible of the promised redemption; what the others had found in the machine the officer had not found; the lips were firmly pressed together, the eyes were open with the same expression as in life, the looks calm and convinced, through the forehead went the point of the great iron spike.

(Kafka, *In the Penal Colony*)

After this, the explorer, the soldier and the now redeemed prisoner return to the town; eventually the explorer leaves the island, in visible disgust at all that he has seen.

Few of Kafka's stories remind us so vividly of his day job, as an insurance clerk dealing with industrial injury claims! This aside, what is Kafka trying to tell us, with such an extraordinary and gruesome tale? Obviously, if it is a 'parable' then we should be wary of trying to pin its meaning down too closely. But for our purposes we can say that this extraordinary tale is about the 'dismantling' of the violent sacred. The officer is proud and protective of his execution machine, which dispenses a justice so perfect and so transcendent that even those being punished are taken up by its radiance. And yet he is concerned that it is losing its force. For reasons that are not made clear, both the governing authorities and the people in general show less and less interest in this 'sacred' procedure, while the machine itself is beginning to creak because it is not being maintained properly. Only the officer really believes in it any more; and when the explorer expresses his disgust, this seems to be the final straw. When the officer places himself on the Harrow, its terminal malfunction is finally made apparent.

We have seen previously what happens when a society needs to preserve or re-establish order within itself. Such a community will have recourse to what Girard calls the scapegoat mechanism: a crisis which has come about because of the uncontrolled activity of mimetic desire is itself resolved by mimetic means. The aggression which is threatening to tear the community apart is rechannelled onto an individual victim or marginal group. This purely social process of expulsion or extermination appears to the perpetrators as if it is a holy action, because it brings, if only temporarily, the peace and harmony which the group desperately needs. Precisely because the sacrifice seems to be efficacious, it must be 'of God'. Even the victim, being simultaneously good and evil, is accorded the status of a primitive deity. Here, once again, is Girard's formulation: 'violence is the heart and secret soul of the sacred'.

The officer's macabre enthusiasm for his execution machine in the Kafka story, and for the 'transcendent' enlightenment it brings about, even in the most hardened criminal, will stand for an illustration of the violent sacred at work. The third phase of Girard's mimetic theory, the subject of this chapter, concerns the role of the Gospel, and of the Bible in general, in disabling this machine and exposing the falsity of the claims to sacredness which are associated with it.

Here is the astonishing 'twist' to the thriller which René Girard has been putting together. His path of discovery brings him to the Bible as a third step (after the discovery of mimetic desire and the scapegoat mechanism), one that follows through on the anthropological questions which have arisen from the first two. The crucial question for Girard is whether the Jewish and Christian religions have their origin in the scapegoat mechanism. He does not deny that many parallels exist between the Bible and myths, or between the Bible and descriptions of religious rites in general. But these, he finally recognises, are far less significant than the Bible's distinctive features.

To begin, however, let us incorporate what has been said so far, by returning to a distinction put forward in Chapter 1, when Girard speaks of the 'Romantic Lie' and 'novelistic truth'. We recall that the novels which interested Girard manifested a pattern of disclosure concerning the truth of mimetic interaction. These writers struggle towards a costly insight, that human desire is configured mimetically. This insight entails a denial of the overriding importance of human autonomy and freedom, whether on philosophical or aesthetic grounds. It is precisely in 'romanticism' that such an insistence occurs, and yet, says Girard, such a world-view operates with a fundamentally mistaken anthropology.

Human individuals and communities are so convinced that they operate autonomously, and are so protective of this autonomy, that they are unaware of the violent measures to which they resort to maintain it. This is the immense power of the social formation called religion, which for Girard is founded on the scapegoating process as a means of establishing order and self-identity, and of maintaining these when they come under threat. For this to work, even temporarily, the persecutors must be ignorant of the innocence of their victim. They must also be ignorant of the mimetic pull which draws them together to eliminate the victim. The different aspects of religion – myth, taboo, ritual – maintain this ignorance.

Myths are for Girard the stories which a religion tells about its origins, though they merely hint at the violence of those origins, rather than declare it outright. The violence of the scapegoating action is often contained in stories of gods doing battle or being sacrificed; but we never find a direct acknowledgement that it is the victimisation of real human beings which is at the heart of these stories. So myths conceal more than they reveal: they are, literally, a 'cover-up'. There is an etymological link to the word 'mute', since myths remain *silent* about the events they purport to describe. Likewise, in Chapter 2 this was framed, by means of Mack's synthesis, as a progression from 'myth' which conceals, to 'literature' which tentatively begins to reveal the truth.

This is as far as Girard has got by the time of *Violence and the Sacred*. With his next work, when Girard looks at the Jewish and Christian scriptures, he wants to insist on a further contrast: between *myth*, in the sense described in the last paragraph, and *gospel*. The Gospel revelation is one which uncovers even more radically the truth which myth seeks to conceal, that is, the murderous interaction of human desires in order to preserve or protect a social order in time of crisis. This revelation occurs gradually, throughout the Old and New Testaments, but finds its clearest expression in the life, teaching, death and resurrection of Jesus, and in the Christian doctrines which reflect upon him.

There is, in other words, an important parallel between the way René Girard has been reading literature, and the way he approaches the biblical text. There is a crucial difference between the 'Romantic Lie' and 'novelistic truth' (between those works of literature which continue to insist on the autonomy of the human self, and those which recognise this to be a dangerous illusion), but there is an even more fundamental gap between myth (covering up the truth of violent human origins) and the Gospel (which exposes and names the scapegoating process for what it is, as well as the false transcendence founded upon it).

Is this the same distinction? For our purposes it is worthwhile to set out Girard's reading of the Bible as another version of the struggle between the Romantic Lie and novelistic truth, precisely in the manner that he reads Proust, Dostoevsky and his other treasured novelists.

That there should be different and opposed ways of reading the Bible comes as a surprise to no one, of course. As William Blake puts it in one of his epigrams, 'Both read the Bible day and night/But thou read'st black where I read white.' In this instance, I would like to propose three general approaches to the biblical text – perhaps we might even want to call them 'grand narratives'. The first, (A), is a relatively neutral telling of the Bible story as it has been read by Christian orthodoxy over the centuries; the second of these 'grand narratives', (B), is a rather breathless composite account of why, for many modern thinkers, the biblical view of God is to be rejected. It is no doubt in need of a great deal of refinement, but the general drift of the argument is familiar enough. (C) is more or less a Girardian understanding of the biblical story.

A. If we read the Bible as a straightforward narrative, it tells the story of God's creation of a good universe. Unfortunately, because of the disobedience of the first humans, a 'fall' takes place, which alienates humanity (and the whole of creation) from the blessed state which God intended for them. This act of disobedience was especially serious because it was an act of illegitimate self-assertion, like that of Satan, by which Adam and Eve attempted to become 'like God'.

As a result, humanity goes into 'free-fall', and all the evils which we now suffer, including violence and death itself, spring from this initial disobedience. The whole of biblical history is a record of God's attempt to put right this catastrophe, first of all by establishing a covenant with a 'chosen' people, who will offer the obedience that was lacking from our first parents by living out the Law entrusted to them.

Even so, a huge theological dilemma remains, which was evident to St Paul and was famously formulated by St Anselm of Canterbury. Human beings are the ones who should mend the damage they have done, but this damage is so extensive that only God is capable of repairing it. Even living a righteous life under the Law will not suffice. There is need of the 'God–Man', Jesus, who comes into the world in order to do what is necessary to put things right (W. H. Auden refers to him as the 'mild engineer'!). In many understandings of salvation, Jesus pays our debt to God, or forestalls the wrath of the Father by, as it were, standing in for us in the dock. His obedience makes up for the disobedience of Adam and Eve (as in Milton's *Paradise Lost* and *Paradise Regained*), and to those who accept his offer of forgiveness and who turn away from sin, there is the promise of new life, which is essentially a restoration of God's original plan for us.

B. The biblical revelation is an enemy of human freedom and flourishing. The God of the Old and New Testaments is just as much a projection of human fears, longings and obsessions as the deities of the Greek and Roman pantheon, and human beings who continue to take him seriously condemn themselves to a state of infantile dependence. Whether we consider the account of the fall in Genesis, or archaic and prohibitive tribal codes such as the Decalogue, it is clear that this 'God' (the figure caricatured by William Blake as 'Nobodaddy') has no interest in people living lives of genuine moral autonomy. Worse, too many of the stories about him reinforce only a despotic and violent patriarchy, which must be rejected in the name of human integrity.

The figure of Jesus in the New Testament, to be sure, does alleviate the picture, as he is a compassionate ethical teacher; but his genuinely human contribution must always stand over against any religious 'truth' as such. Jesus stands on the side of humanity against religion. This is confirmed by the fact that religious leaders could not tolerate his subversive message and cultic transgressions, and had him put to death.

A rejection of the tenets of biblical faith, along these lines, would lie at the heart of most critiques of religion since the Enlightenment. The declaration that belief in God is a matter of projection is, of course, to be found in Feuerbach, Marx and Freud, while the tension between autonomous morality and religious revelation as incompatible grounds for human conduct is explored by Kant, especially in his reading of the sacrifice of Abraham. For Nietzsche, even the possibility that the prophetic compassion of Jesus might represent a more acceptable face of the Judaeo–Christian code is rejected, since Jesus is the embodiment of 'slave morality' based on *ressentiment*. Each of these readings offers a 'hermeneutic of suspicion' which delivers the same message: there is a fundamental opposition between God and the human family, so that for the sake of human well-being we have to reject the biblical revelation and its God. (The fantasy novels of Philip Pullman, who makes no secret of his antipathy towards organised religion, are a popular current manifestation of this style of thinking.)

C. For Girard, it is precisely because of the human tendency towards projection and false transcendence that the biblical revelation is necessary. The fullness of this revelation is found in the Easter message: when we adjust our eyes to its strange light, we see a radically different story to the second account, and even to the first in important respects. Biblical history is the history of one true, loving God, urging us to cast aside false idols and to live in the truth – and the most important of the untruths which must be rejected is the false transcendence which issues from our conflictive desires and our negotiation of them through sacred violence. The entirety of the biblical revelation is nothing less than God's struggle to lead his people towards this new awareness, one that will indeed 'set them apart' from the other nations. The face of the true God is gradually but inexorably revealed as infinitely loving, and completely beyond all violence.

This is evidenced in key moments of biblical history, in the commandments and legislative codes which seek to restrain or renounce mimesis and violence. The Old Testament climax of this process of revelation occurs with the figure of the Servant of Yahweh, in Isaiah, who seems to be a scapegoat for the people, but is shown to be the Lord's anointed, and whose sufferings are read by Christians as prefiguring those of Christ. In the New Testament, it is the preaching of Christ, affirmed by his death and resurrection, which manifest the truth of God as loving Father with even greater clarity. Jesus insists throughout on the link between distorted desire and violent self-affirmation, and he is especially critical of a religious system which masks this connection and refuses to take responsibility for it. Only by confronting this system directly can the full murderous force of the scapegoating process be exposed and made ineffective. Only then is the true face of God revealed.

There can be, in short, no genuine opposition – no 'metaphysical rivalry', to use Girard's term – between God and humanity. It is a mistake to conceive of relations between God and man as a Hegelian dialectic between Master and Slave – even if modernity and its great thinkers persist in precisely this view of the matter. In so far as men and women align themselves with the true God, and with his project for humanity, they live in the truth. If, however, they insist on affirming their independence and autonomy over against God, they are perpetuating a religious version of the 'Romantic Lie', one which offers no escape from the vicious spiral of desire and violence. Such a false affirmation of humanity can only lead to humanity's self-destruction.

Those familiar with the hermeneutics of Paul Ricœur may want to see in these three readings the familiar pattern of 'first naiveté/critique/second naiveté', and in many respects Girard's theory is an attempt to read the Bible afresh in the light of the criticisms of the 'masters of suspicion', such as Freud and Nietzsche. What follows is a consideration of some of the biblical passages which offer themselves for this fresh reading. From the huge amount of material which could be cited here, the following six passages and episodes are among the most significant. I will examine each briefly, and draw them together by summing up Girard's Christianity as essentially Johannine. In fact, it can be said that Girard's fundamental anthropology is a reflection upon a single biblical citation, John

11:49–51, which declares, with typical Johannine ambiguity, that Jesus both is, and is not, a scapegoat:

> One of them, Caiaphas, the high priest that year, said, 'You don't seem to have grasped the situation at all; you fail to see that it is better for one man to die for the people, than for the whole nation to be destroyed.' He did not speak in his own person, it was as high priest that he made this prophecy that Jesus was to die for the nation – and not for the nation only, but to gather together in unity the scattered children of God.

(a) The Narrative of the Fall (Genesis 1—4)

The early chapters of Genesis link three events which should be seen in causal sequence: the fall of Adam and Eve, after they had disobeyed the injunction not to eat of the fruit; the death of Abel at the hands of his brother Cain; and the destruction of the world by means of the Flood. The initial gesture of appropriation by the first couple (as a result, it should be noted, of a desire mediated to them by the serpent) is the prologue to worse disasters: to the death of Abel, who is murdered as a result of his brother's envious revenge, and then to the widespread chaos and undifferentiation into which human society collapses before the Flood. Even the murder of Abel, in fact, has a mimetic interpretation. Girard offers the intriguing explanation, that in fact both the brothers are potentially murderous, but that Abel has a 'safety-valve' through animal sacrifice, which Cain does not have – and so the latter's aggression is vented onto his brother.

Like Romulus, slayer of his brother Remus, Cain is the founder of culture: he is 'the builder of a town'. Nevertheless, the condemnation of Cain by God distinguishes this story from the Roman myth, which largely justifies the fratricide. At the same time, God places a mark upon Cain which is intended to distinguish him and to discourage further mimetic violence.

(b) Abraham and Isaac (Genesis 22)

The story of how Abraham is called upon by God to sacrifice his only son Isaac, as a test of his faith, is certainly a difficult and highly problematic narrative. Feminist critic Phyllis Trible has referred to this and similar stories in the Old Testament as 'texts of terror'. Immanuel Kant insisted that no command of God can or should be respected if it goes against the moral law, and here Abraham is quite clearly being asked to perform an immoral action. Even within the Christian tradition, there is something very frightening about this text which is usually presented as a celebration of Abraham, 'our father in faith', in apparent neglect of the fact that at its heart is the proposed slaying of a young boy. How could a loving God put anyone to the test in this horrible fashion?

The story looks different, however, if we look at its likely pedagogical intent, which is that of pulling Israelites away from the practice of human, and specifically child sacrifice; a cult still carried out by their neighbours, and one which the Israelites themselves may have renounced only with the greatest of difficulty. If this is what is going on, then a drama which sets out the fact of God's disapproval of this form of sacrifice is in fact a very important anthropological 'trace'. Within the text as we have it, there are clear hints of changes that have taken place in the course of the editing – even to the point of there being two different names for God! 'Elohim' orders the sacrifice, but the command which cancels it comes from 'Yahweh'. A further sign of the text being edited, but without totally removing the traces of human sacrifice, is the fact that Abraham comes down the mountain alone in verse 19. As one scholar, Bruce Vawter, has put it, we should read this text with the 'generosity' its authors intended. Abraham arrives at a new conception of what is pleasing to God, even a new conception of God himself. This obscure shrine in the desert is here being commemorated as the place where it was brought into the heart of man not only that God preferred obedience to sacrifice, but also that there were some sacrifices he did not want at all:

> It would be surprising were there no record at all, no awareness shown, of the development that once took place in religious history, of the new insight that was afforded into the nature of God and his requirements, which accounts for such diametrically opposed outlooks on human sacrifice as that of Israel on the one hand and that of the rest of its cultural world on the other. We can suggest that Genesis 22:1–14 may be read as the record of

such a development, or at least a part of it ... If we must resist the temptation to read into these stories more than they intended to say or other than they intended to say, we must also not succumb to the opposite temptation to hold their meaning to the paltry and parsimonious when they would have it generous. Israel did, after all, almost alone of its compeers raise its eyes to a vision of God and religion that relegated the otherwise respectable institution of human sacrifice to the dank backwaters of superstition and barbarism. It ought not seem strange that its great forefather Abraham should have been thought to anticipate this enlargement of the human spirit even as he has anticipated so much else that is Israelite in the pages of Genesis.

(Vawter, 1977, p. 256)

(c) Joseph and His Brothers (Genesis 37)

The account of the sufferings of Joseph at the hands of his brothers has for Girard the character of a fully visible persecution myth. He speculates that here, as elsewhere (for example, Isaac's blessing of Jacob), the biblical writers have recast a pre-existent mythology for their own purposes. In fact, the pre-existent story is inverted, as is the relationship between the victim and the persecuting community. Joseph is nearly put to death, but he escapes; the animal which is killed in order to create the impression of Joseph's death is a substitute. There are even echoes of the Oedipus myth, since Potiphar is really a substitute father to Joseph, and so the accusation of Potiphar's wife has an incestuous connotation. In the story as a whole, the rehabilitation of the victim (first Joseph, then Benjamin) and not his sacralisation, means that the sacral effects of the scapegoating process do not occur. Joseph is neither demonised nor divinised, but remains human – and by pardoning his brothers he is able to found a non-violent conviviality with them.

(d) The Servant of Yahweh

In contrast to the tendency of the scapegoating mentality, many texts from the Old Testament manifest a partiality for the persecuted victim. This theme recurs in the Psalms, in the prophetic writings, and in the dialogues in the book of Job. The high point of the Old Testament in this respect has to be the four Servant Songs of Second Isaiah (Isaiah 42:1–9; 49:1–6; 50:4–11; 52:13—53:12). They describe the fate of the Servant of Yahweh, who is attacked and insulted by men. 'The most striking aspect here, the trait which is certainly unique, is the innocence of the Servant, the fact that he has no connection with violence and no affinity for it' (Girard, 1987a, p. 157). His fate is identical with that of the scapegoat:

> By force and by law he was taken;
> would anyone plead his cause?
> Yes, he was torn away from the land of the living;
> for our faults he was struck down in death.
> They gave him a grave with the wicked,
> a tomb with the rich,
> though he had done no wrong
> and there had been no perjury in his mouth.
>
> (Isaiah 53:8–9)

These last lines are decisive; the innocence of the Servant is upheld, as the speaker takes his side. There is also a departure from the typical mythical-religious judgement that the victim is being punished by God; here this aspect of the scapegoat mechanism is uncovered:

> But we, we thought of him as someone punished,
> struck by God and brought low.
> Yet he was pierced through for our faults,
> crushed for our sins.
>
> (Isaiah 53:4–5)

We have texts, therefore, which reveal the scapegoat mechanism and take the part of the victim. The 'dialogue' between God, the Servant and the people resembles the interchange between characters and Chorus in a Greek drama. Whether the 'Servant' is a collective identity (e.g. the people of Israel) or an individual one is immaterial, as either would allow for a mimetic interpretation: 'all nations against Israel' is structurally the same event as a crowd of evildoers against one individual. As Raymund Schwager makes clear, nowhere in the text of Second Isaiah is there a prayer for revenge on one's enemies, such as we find in Jeremiah or in many psalms. It is this absence of the theme of vengeance, so widespread in the Old Testament, that alerts us to something very new in the Servant's non-violent behaviour.

In the fourth Song, the same people who perpetrated his punishment now come to recognise that the Servant suffered vicariously for the many (53:4–12). Victimisers recognise the consequence of their persecution; there is also the upsetting of the normal mechanism, by which the crimes of evildoers fall back upon the perpetrators. Instead, an innocent person is struck vicariously. The servant's free acceptance of these misdeeds has two effects: it ensures that they do not fall back on the heads of the perpetrators as vengeance, and it therefore enables them to come to a greater understanding of their actions. How this awareness comes about is not explicit, but it seems to be the non-violence of the victim which opens their eyes: 'Because he carried the offences of the many for all to behold, he became a light for the nations. By empowering his servant to adopt a new attitude, God at the same time revealed himself in a new way' (Schwager, 1987, p. 133).

(e) The Teachings of Jesus and His Prophetic Critique of Religion

The Sermon on the Mount gives examples of how the teachings familiar to Jesus from his Jewish tradition are radicalised, so as to combat mimetic conflict at its very source: the desires of the heart. It is not just that murder and adultery are wrong, but the appetites which lead to these actions, namely anger and lust, are also to be acknowledged and controlled. Jesus exhorts his followers to actions of renunciation which can break the cycle of retributive violence, such as turning the other cheek, walking the extra mile, and so on. Even to a believer, these look the height of madness and weakness; and yet, says Girard, in our modern world, which has lost its capacity to channel and control violence safely, such prescriptions begin to make a terrifying sense.

Many of the actions of Jesus bear out this call to unconditional love, such as his forgiveness of sins and his table fellowship with sinners. Parables such as the Lost Sheep (who is sought out by the shepherd, even as he leaves 99 sheep untended) are a reversal of the scapegoat mentality, which is readier to sacrifice the individual for the sake of the majority. In *The Scapegoat* Girard has a powerful reading of Mark's version of the Gerasene demoniac (Mark 5), which is to be read as a mirror-image of a scapegoat persecution. By the end of this story, the tormented man is sitting at the top of the cliff, clothed and in his right mind, while the community which had been persecuting him ('we are Legion') has been symbolically 'cast out' in the form of the pigs who are sent over the cliff. Not surprisingly, given the turbulence this has caused to their exclusionary social arrangements, the villagers themselves are scared of Jesus, and ask him to leave the district.

It is in his confrontation with the scribes and Pharisees that the significance of Jesus' critique of the scapegoat process is most evident. It helps to explain why his polemic against the religious leaders is so fierce: their refusal to acknowledge the persecutory violence which is at the heart of their religious observance means that they will continue to be complicit in crimes committed in the name of their religion. When the leaders insist that 'we would never have persecuted the prophets in the way our fathers did' (Matt. 23:30), they deceive themselves, and they remain entrapped in the cycle of violence. 'Woe to you! For you build the tombs of the prophets whom your fathers killed!' (Matt. 23:29). They are therefore responsible for the deaths of all the prophets who have been murdered, from Abel to Zechariah – the A–Z of victimisation. Their denial of complicity means they are 'whited sepulchres', presenting an acceptable face to the deathly corruption within. In an even more sinister insult, Jesus accuses the scribes of being 'unmarked graves', walked over by men who have not the faintest idea about the victims underfoot.

Such criticisms by Jesus of the religious authorities are unequivocal. What is less clear is the extent to which they can be linked to the anti-cultic or anti-sacrificial elements in Jesus' teaching. These are certainly present: Jesus himself quotes the prophet Hosea, that God requires mercy and not sacrifice (Hosea 6:6; Matt. 9:13; 12:7), and he emphatically relativises prescriptions concerning sabbath observance and ritual purity. It is easy to overplay such indicators, however, and as we shall see, arguments about the legitimacy of the language of 'sacrifice' with reference to Christ loom large in the development of mimetic theory. In any case, at the time of writing *Things Hidden* Girard was convinced that Jesus' prophetic stance against cultic action as such was to be understood as a part of his strategy against scapegoating.

(f) The Passion and Resurrection

The Passion narratives stand at the centre of the New Testament in Girard's theory. The New Testament recognises in Jesus an unjustly persecuted scapegoat, though the expression used is the 'Lamb of God'. With this theme, Jesus is identified with the figure of the Suffering Servant in Second Isaiah, as well as other texts in the Jewish scriptures, where the viewpoint of the victim is taken up and the scapegoat mechanism unveiled. Girard reads the stoning of Stephen, the first Christian martyr, in the same way.

This unveiling happens as a kind of dramatic enactment. Here, we may draw on the account of Raymund Schwager, one of Girard's most important theological collaborators, whose *Jesus im Heilsdrama (Jesus and the Drama of Salvation)* sets out a presentation of Jesus' role in five acts, as it were: Act I opens with Jesus' offer of unconditional divine forgiveness and salvation to Israel; Act II includes both the negative public response to Jesus' summons to repent, and Jesus' reaction to the general rejection of his message. This second act presents the crisis, leading to the central Act III, which is a presentation and interpretation of the crucifixion.

Jesus' proclamation of the kingdom has not produced the collective response he had expected. It appears that his mission has ended in failure, and that disaster will once again overtake the people of Israel. He therefore symbolically completes his mission to Israel through the cleansing of the temple, and now offers his life as an act of atonement for the collective force of human sin. Crucial to the transition between the acts here is the disturbing parable of the vineyard, which appears in all three synoptic gospels. From Isaiah 5, Jesus' listeners would know that the 'man constructing a vineyard' refers unambiguously to God's relationship with Israel:

> A man planted a vineyard; he fenced it round, dug out a trough for the winepress and built a tower; then he leased it to tenants and went abroad. When the time came, he sent a servant to the tenants to collect from them his share of the produce of the vineyard. But they seized the man, thrashed him and sent him away empty handed. Next he sent another servant to them; him they beat about the head and treated shamefully. And he sent another and him they killed; then a number of others, and they thrashed

some and killed the rest. He had still someone left: his beloved son. He sent him to them last of all, thinking, 'They will respect my son.' But those tenants said to each other: 'This is the heir. Come on, let us kill him, and the inheritance will be ours.' So they seized him and killed him and threw him out of the vineyard. Now what will the owner of the vineyard do?

(Mark 12:1–8)

In Mark and Luke's versions of the parable, Jesus answers his own question; in Matthew the answer is put in the mouth of his hearers: 'He will come and put the tenants to death, and give the vineyard to others.' In all three, the parable is followed by Jesus reminding his audience of Psalm 118, a psalm of thanksgiving: 'the stone which the builders rejected has become the cornerstone: this is what the Lord has done, a marvel in our eyes' (Ps. 118:22-23).

Even as the events of Holy Week unfold, and Jesus becomes more isolated, still he persists in 'enacting' God's unconditional love through such gestures as the institution of the Eucharist at the Last Supper, and finally by dying on the cross, without ever crying out for vengeance on his enemies. And yet he dies as a 'scapegoat', with everyone ranged against him: 'Herod and Pontius Pilate made an alliance with the pagan nations and the peoples of Israel' against Jesus (Acts 4:27) – even his friends take part, indirectly, in this alliance, since they all desert Jesus or betray him. The judgement passed upon Jesus is a human deed, not a divine act. Nevertheless, he is killed and buried, and the truth of Jesus' message remains an open question, one which can only be answered by an act of God.

In Act IV, this ambivalence is marvellously resolved, with the resurrection as the conclusive judgement of the heavenly Father. For Schwager the resurrection encompasses two things: first, a divine judgement in favour of the crucified Jesus; secondly, an astonishing advance to a new and unexpected stage of God's self-revelation. What God does, in raising Jesus from the dead, is a completely unexpected contrast to the anticipated actions of the owner in the parable of the vineyard. Not only does God refrain from vengeance, he even forgives the murder of his Son, and opens up a new avenue of reconciliation for his killers: 'a mercy greater than which none can be conceived'.

Finally, Act V of Raymund Schwager's dramatic scheme deals with the descent of the Holy Spirit at Pentecost, and the new gathering of the Church. The Spirit is operative above all in the internal transformation of individuals and in the new assembly. Jesus' initial efforts to gather Israel failed, but the sending of the Holy Spirit is a 'second wave' of the Father's invitation. Through the Spirit (called *Paraclete*, a Greek word meaning, among other things, the advocate for the defence), God is able to reach and transform the innermost core of the human heart, by the celebration of the Eucharist and by a deeper understanding in faith. Another word for this understanding is: the intelligence of the Victim, the new perspective that is in place as Christians become aware of what has happened and of how God has finally broken through to them.

We have considered six passages from the Old and New Testaments which appear to offer evidence for a mimetic reading of the biblical text. There are countless others which have been used, either by Girard himself or other scholars. For example, Girard has written on the book of Job as a scapegoating narrative, while the story of the prophet Jonah exhibits many of the aspects of the scapegoating process, as well as a way out of it. Girard's reading of the Decalogue in *I Saw Satan Fall like Lightning* offers a fresh view of the Ten Commandments, as a way of limiting the conflict that can issue from mimetic desire. In all of these narratives there are hints, more or less strong, of how a way out of the spiral of violent retribution may be found, towards a community built on non-rivalrous conviviality – though only with God's help, and only through personal and communal conversion. Whatever else one makes of Girard's mimetic theory, there is no doubt that it has yielded, from Girard and others, readings of the biblical texts of sometimes astonishing power and creativity.

The whole biblical drama, for Girard, is nothing less than the kind of struggle towards conversion and enlightenment that we find in Proust and Dostoevsky, though obviously on a far vaster scale. The content of the conversion is the same: a radical change of perspective, which emerges when the subject is confronted with the reality of its own imitated desire, its ontological emptiness, and the violence which issues from it. It is the moment of realisation which is expressed in Acts, when Peter preaches to the stunned crowd: 'God has made him Lord and Messiah, this Jesus whom you crucified':

When they heard this, they were struck to the heart and said to Peter and the Apostles: 'What should we do, brothers?' Peter answered them: 'Repent, and let each of you be baptised in the name of Jesus Christ, for the forgiveness of sins; then you will receive the gift of the Holy Spirit.'

(Acts 2:37–38)

In so far as the content of the earliest Christian preaching can be discerned, the shock of the reversal of Jesus' fate – the stone which the builders rejected has become the cornerstone – is central to it. Here, as elsewhere, great significance is given to the fact that the persecutors acted unknowingly. Peter, once again:

The God of Abraham, Isaac and Jacob, the God of our Fathers, has glorified his Servant Jesus, whom you betrayed and denied before Pilate, although he had decided to let him go. You, however, denied the Holy and Righteous One, and allowed a murderer to go free. You have killed the Author of life, but God has raised him from the dead. To this we are witnesses ... now brothers, I know that you acted out of ignorance, just like your leaders. God, however, has fulfilled in this way what he prophesied through the mouths of all the prophets: that his Chosen One would have to suffer.

(Acts 3:13–15, 17–18)

The scope of Girard's claims for a mimetic reading of the gospels can be appreciated further if we compare the opening chapter of Genesis, and the Prologue of the Gospel of John. Each tell of what took place 'in the beginning': 'the prologue to John shows the whole Bible being *recommenced* from the point of view of the Logos as victim' (Girard, 1987a, p. 274). The Fall narrative of Genesis tells of a good creation which starts to go awry because of an act of appropriation by Adam and Eve. It is not simply that the fruit itself is desirable as an object: what it signifies, the knowledge of good and evil, and therefore a share in the very Being of God, makes this an example of 'metaphysical' and not just 'acquisitive' mimesis. In any case, the fruit is eaten, and the sad scene follows in which recriminations are cast, including the suggestion that God is not entirely blameless from all of this (Adam slyly asserts that 'the woman *you gave me* tempted me'). There are punishments and an expulsion: the couple are cast out of Paradise – it would appear as a pre-emptive measure by God, in case they eat of the Tree of Life and become even more of a rival to him. No one comes out of this too well, and certainly not God.

If we turn to the Prologue of John, however, what we find is a re-writing of the Genesis narrative – from God's perspective, as it were, therefore from a perspective which has nothing in it of mimetic anxiety or retributive vengeance. 'The Johannine Logos is foreign to any kind of violence; it is therefore forever expelled, an absent Logos that never has had any direct determining influence over human cultures' (1987a, p. 271). Such cultures are founded on the other 'logos' of Greek philosophy, which only knows 'strife as the king and father of all things'. Where the Genesis narrative sets up a rivalry between God and the human beings created by him, the Prologue assures us that those who believe in Christ are invited to become 'children of God'. In other words, the very identity which Adam and Eve snatched at in Genesis is here being offered as a free gift.

Like the Genesis narrative, John's Prologue tells of an expulsion, but here it is not human beings who are cast out by God. On the contrary, it is the Word, the light of all men, who is not received by the world – 'his own knew him not'. To put this even more starkly: the 'non-receiving' of the Word is, of course, the act of violent rejection which is the Crucifixion. Once again, we have *l'envers du mythe*: a mythological account is turned inside out or redirected. For all the evasiveness which we find in the Genesis narratives (Cain denying responsibility for his murdered brother), the Prologue makes plain the true origin and direction of violence, once and for all.

There is a further Johannine refinement to the argument here. In the fourth gospel, the moment of Jesus' death is also the hour of his glory, when his true identity is revealed. In other words, it is only as the Lamb of God that the true face of God can be apprehended in the world – at the very moment of his expulsion. This occurs in Mark's gospel also, when the centurion declares Jesus to be the Son of God, even as he dies on the cross. It is precisely at the moment of expulsion, and only then, that God is revealed.

The upshot of this is that God can *never* be recognised as one of the persecutors. God is emphatically denied all involvement with violent actions. Even the resurrection must be read as his declaration of his absolute non-involvement with violent death, much less with the retribution which one would expect to follow the massacre of his Son. Yet, only by 'acting out' the Passion, and taking the part of the innocent victim, was Jesus able to initiate the process of traumatic conversion, one which enabled those who 'know not what they do' to be enlightened, and to have a change of heart.

In order to bring about a true unveiling of the mechanisms of violence, Jesus must be completely independent from the world, and his insight into the logic of violence can only come from 'outside' the world. Girard speaks here of a transcendence which is quite different from the false transcendence brought about by the scapegoat process. The Godhead of Jesus does not result from his sacralisation as a scapegoat on the cross; rather, he is 'from all eternity begotten of God'. Because Jesus has his origin not in the will of man, nor urge of the flesh, but in God, a perfect non-violent love is a possibility for him. For this reason, Girard finds a new meaning in the doctrine of the virginal conception of Jesus. If we compare the nativity accounts in Matthew and Luke with the scurrilous and violent pagan 'myths' about divine relations with women, we see how the Christian doctrine emphasises Jesus' distance from the world of coercion in which men (and false deities) have their origins.

Girard and Nietzsche

All of this, for Girard, argues for the uniqueness of Christianity. Nowhere else does he find expressed so clearly and comprehensively the anthropological insights he has been struggling towards as he does in the Bible, and as this realisation takes root he becomes fiercely 'protective' of Christianity, in so far as the desire to differentiate it from other religious perspectives becomes an overriding concern for him. This leads to a certain amount of ambivalence in his discussion of sacrifice. However, the text which enabled him to articulate a solution to this problem of the difference between the biblical perspective and a more general religious one, comes not from a Christian source, but from Friedrich Nietzsche.

We have already seen from Chapter 1 that Girard's understanding of mimetic desire requires an overview of the theme of *ressentiment*. Here, it is Nietzsche's obsession with Christianity and its alternative which concerns him, a theme which is comparatively neglected by contemporary scholars. For Girard, this neglect is a truncation of what is 'really exciting and novel in the Nietzschean corpus'; in particular, Nietzsche's assertion of the uniqueness of Christianity, precisely because it comes from an anti-Christian perspective, needs to be taken seriously. The relationship between the cult of Dionysus and a disturbing, necessary violence is mentioned in *The Birth of Tragedy*, but the text which attracts Girard's attention is an unpublished fragment, relating to aphorism no. 1052 in *The Will to Power* (1888):

> Dionysus versus the 'Crucified'; there is the antithesis. It is *not* a difference with regard to their martyrdom, it is a difference with regard to the meaning of it. Life itself, its eternal fruitfulness and recurrence, creates anguish, destruction, the will to annihilation . . . On the other hand, suffering, the 'Crucified as the Innocent One', counts as an objection to this life, as a formula for its condemnation. One can guess that the problem is the meaning of suffering: either a Christian sense or a tragic sense . . . In the first case, it is supposed to be the way to a holy existence, in the second case existence is already *holy enough* to justify even an immensity of suffering. The tragic man affirms even the harshest suffering: he is strong, complete, deifying enough for this. The Christian man denies even the happiest state on earth; he is weak, poor, disinherited enough to suffer, no matter what the condition of life . . . 'The God on the Cross' is a curse upon life, a hint as to how one can save oneself from it. Dionysus, cut into pieces, is a promise of Life: it will be reborn eternally and return from annihilation.

Elsewhere Nietzsche further specifies the difference brought about by the Christian Gospel's victory over an 'outlawed human love':

> The particular historical working of Christianity consists in the elevation of egoism, the individual – egoism unto the extreme, the extreme of the individual's immortality. Through Christianity the particular has become so important, so absolute, that one can no longer *sacrifice:* this does not simply mean human sacrifice . . . the outlawed human love desires the sacrifice to the best of the species –

it is hard, it is full of willpower, because it requires human sacrifice. And this pseudo-humanity called Christianity wishes to bring it about that *no one will be sacrificed.*

There are two types of religion therefore: one which is prepared to accept even the most severe degree of suffering, for the sake of the higher values which are thus preserved or brought into being, and one which rejects suffering and seeks to overcome it. Nietzsche sides with Dionysus, and holds the Bible and Christianity responsible for the destruction of all culture. As Girard asserts, this makes Christianity 'anti-pagan'. Nietzsche is to be valued for his resistance to all 'fundamentally anti-biblical' efforts to turn mythology into a kind of Bible (which is what Jungians do), or to dissolve the Bible into mythology (which is what most other people do).

Nevertheless, as Girard has declared in an interview: 'I would describe myself in a way as against – or anti – Nietzsche.' He refuses to gloss over the unpleasant and untenable consequences of Nietzsche's espousal of mythological violence in his later writings: an espousal which, for Girard, makes Nietzsche's current fashion-ability as a philosopher, a teacher of ethics, or a 'lifestyle' guide a par-ticularly irresponsible one. The greatness of Nietzsche consists less in the positive content of his thought, than in his having recognised the truth of Christianity in an incomparable way, and in his being 'deeply but paradoxically involved' in the process of making gener-ative violence increasingly intelligible. Like Caiaphas, he is the unwitting spokesperson for this process, which is impelled by the biblical revelation.

CHAPTER 4

Method and Objections

If there is a 'beatific vision' in Girard's writing (or, to return to the metaphor of the 'spy thriller' used in the Introduction, a moment when all the clues fall into place at last), this would probably be in Girard's discussion, in *A Theatre of Envy*, of the statue scene at the end of *The Winter's Tale*. Here, according to Girard, is the moment where the humanity of Shakespeare shines through, and also where, for the first time in Shakespeare's drama, 'a transcendental perspective silently opens up'.

The climax of the play sees King Leontes contemplating what he believes is a statue of his dead wife, Hermione. Because his vicious jealousy led to her death and that of their daughter (as he believes), he is torn apart with remorse for what he has destroyed. At this point the statue, which is the real Hermione all along, 'comes to life', and a reconciliation is achieved. Girard is not the only critic to see the motif of resurrection here, but the scene is used by him as a powerful illustration of what the 'conversion = resurrection' experience of mimetic theory actually means. First of all, he sets this in the context of his previous writing:

> In my work on the European novel I found that in all major novelists there exists one key work, sometimes two, or even more, whose conclusions, although far from uniform, all belong to the same easily recognizable group because they all reproduce the death and resurrection pattern. This pattern is banal and may signify very little, but it may also refer to the experience I have just defined, so fundamental to the greatness of great works and so powerful that the creators are irresistibly led to allude to it, generally at the place in the work that is best suited to the purpose, the conclusion. In *Deceit, Desire and the Novel* I named these significant conclusions *conversions romanesques*

– a misleading label, I am afraid, since this phenomenon transcends all literary distinctions, including distinctions of genre.

(Girard, 1991, p. 339)

His reading of the statue scene itself plays on the notion of 'stone': the stone of Hermione's 'statue'; the hearts of stone which God promises to Ezekiel to replace with hearts of flesh; the *skandalon* or stumbling-block mentioned by Jesus, and which Girard uses as a technical term for a mimetic obstacle; the stones which are hurled onto the victim by the gathered community – or, conversely, which they set down, 'beginning with the eldest'. There are also the two stones which refer directly to the gospel resurrection narratives: the heavy stone placed over the tomb of Jesus; and the celebration of Jesus as the stone rejected by the builders, which has become the cornerstone. The resonances of this single word, taken together, provide all the elements of mimetic theory.

> What makes our hearts turn to stone is the discovery that, in one sense or another, we are all butchers pretending to be sacrificers. When we understand this, the *skandalon* that we had always managed to discharge upon some scapegoat becomes our own responsibility, a stone as unbearably heavy upon our hearts as Jesus himself upon the saint's shoulders in the Christopher legend.
>
> One thing alone can put an end to this infernal ordeal, the certainty of being forgiven. This is what Leontes is granted when he finally sees that Hermione is being returned to him alive. This is the first such miracle in Shakespeare; it was still spectacularly impossible at the end of *King Lear*, but now comes to pass for the first time. As the statue turns from stone to flesh, so does the heart of Leontes.
>
> The model for this conclusion can only be the Gospel itself, interpreted as this dissolving of the *skandalon* just evoked. Shakespeare must have recognized in the Gospels the true revelation not only of God but of man, of what his mimetic imprisonment makes of man. His genius, and more than his genius, enabled Shakespeare to recapture in this conclusion something that belongs exclusively to the

Gospels, the nonmagical and yet nonnaturalistic quality of their resurrection. The more we examine the statue scene, the more we are reminded of what that resurrection is supposed to be, a resurrection of the flesh, in contradistinction to the vaporous world of spirits conjured up by mimetic idolatry. The delayed recognition of Jesus has nothing to do with a lesser visibility of his resurrected body due to the lesser reality of the shadowy afterlife to which he now would belong. The opposite is true. This resurrection is too real for a perception dimmed by the false transfigurations of mimetic idolatry.

(Girard, 1991, pp. 341–2)

The deep joyful simplicity of this scene should remind us that the basic elements of mimetic theory are not all that difficult to grasp. They chart a movement from conflictual desire and exclusionary violence, to conversion, resurrection and forgiveness – though what is most surprising is to see this biblical language being used as literary criticism.

Nevertheless, Girard is adamant that these fundamental insights can be scientifically and philosophically grounded. As one critic puts it, 'the necessity of the kingdom of God becomes scientific'. Because of this, discussion of Girard's 'system' soon becomes extremely complex. The present chapter will be more abstract than the preceding ones, as it attempts both to deepen our understanding of Girard's theory, and to some extent try to see it whole – without, in other words, losing sight of the 'beatific vision'. We will elucidate some of the methodological issues raised by Girard's thinking, and in the process look at some of the objections that have been brought forward against it.

The third of Girard's major works, certainly his most extensive, appeared in the French original in 1978. *Things Hidden Since the Foundation of the World* is set out as a series of discussions between Girard and two psychoanalysts. It is not an easy book to read; even so, the basic elements of mimetic theory are all present. What the text does seek to do is to situate these insights in a wider scientific and philosophical context. Girard has published extensively since *Things Hidden*, as a glance at the bibliography will make clear. Nevertheless, with the publication of this work, after *Desire, Deceit and the Novel* and *Violence and the Sacred*, all the tenets of mimetic theory were now in explicit and published form, making possible an overall assessment of Girard's life-work.

It will be clear why Girard's theory is a *skandalon* to many, since he cuts across the grain of so many intellectual prejudices. To take the most obvious, academic specialists are not unreasonably prickly about the brashness of a theorist who lays claim to explanatory power in anthropology, psychology, literary criticism, biblical studies and theology (even if, for the theory's supporters, this interdisciplinary promiscuity is precisely its most attractive feature). In itself, perhaps this is not so unusual, as much of contemporary cultural theory does the same kind of thing. On the other hand, Girard's theory is an explicit challenge to certain trends within postmodern thinking, not least because of his explicit allegiance to Christianity, which puts him at the margin of French and American academic establishments.

Girard's self-described 'obsession' with a limited number of literary and cultural themes, making of him a 'hedgehog thinker', does mean that a great deal tends to be excluded or taken for granted in his writing. Hostile critics will find no shortage of passages where he seems to overreach himself. Once again, it is often the case that in Girard's interviews we come across important nuances to his thinking. I would suggest seven areas of concern or interest, though will not deal with each to the same extent. Two may be described as methodological in the broad sense:

1. The theoretical status of mimetic theory
2. Girard and philosophy

There are specific questions to be put to the theory itself:

3. The anthropology of the scapegoat mechanism
4. Girard and historical Christianity
5. Girard's 'gnosticism'

And finally, two specific appraisals of mimetic theory:

6. Theological critique: Girard, Schwager and Balthasar
7. Feminist reception of mimetic theory

1. Can this be called a theory?

We should address the basic question of just what kind of body of knowledge is being presented to us. What we explored as a series of integrated insights is variously described by Girard and others as a 'hypothesis' and a 'theory'. Clearly, Girard understands himself to be putting forward claims which in some sense have the status of scientific propositions. If we are to assess these claims, some clarity about vocabulary is needed. A Dictionary of Philosophy (Lacey, 1976) defines 'hypothesis' as 'a statement not yet accepted as true, or as a law', in which case it may be better not to speak of the mimetic 'hypothesis', as Girard sometimes does, because this is a cluster of insights which are not reducible to a 'single statement'. Lacey offers several definitions of 'theory', which sometimes shade into one another:

> (i) One or more hypotheses or lawlike statements . . . regarded as speculative. (ii) A law about unobservables like electrons or evolution, sometimes called a theory because evidence about unobservables is felt to be inevitably inconclusive. (iii) A unified system of laws or hypotheses, with explanatory force (not merely like a railway timetable). (iv) A field of study (e.g. in philosophy: theory of knowledge, logical theory).

On the first definition, 'theory' and 'hypothesis' are interchangeable. Definition (iv) would presumably apply, but tell us not very much. Definitions (ii) and (iii) look promising: proponents of the mimetic system certainly regard it as 'a unified system of laws or hypotheses, with explanatory force'. At the same time, the system deals to some extent with 'unobservables', in two senses: first, the anthropological or ethnological evidence which would make good its claims about the origins of primitive societies is difficult to obtain, and secondly, the scapegoating mechanism operates unseen and covers its traces by means of prohibitions, myths, rituals and so on, so that its presence can only be a matter of inferral.

This is important, since one of the objections raised against Girard's system is the lack of evidence for it. This is just what the theory would lead us to expect. Myth is the 'muteness' which shrouds in silence the truth about scapegoats and victimhood. In this sense the scapegoat mechanism resembles the idea of the 'unconscious' in psychoanalysis or, as mentioned above, the way electrons or evolution are used in scientific discourse.

In *The Gospel and the Sacred*, Robert Hamerton-Kelly agrees with the legitimacy of positing the existence of unobservables as a form of 'scientific realism'. He is confident that 'the scientific status of the theory of sacred violence is secure within the context of responsible debate within the philosophy of science' (Hamerton-Kelly, 1994, p. 44), and goes on to offer his own understanding of what 'theory' is and does. Theory, according to Hamerton-Kelly, is above all a moment of creative insight which guides our looking, one which cannot therefore be arrived at by induction. Hypotheses are proposed and tested in the search for laws – laws are in fact proved hypotheses. On the other hand:

> Theories are tested differently, not by the reliability of correlations but by their power and elegance. According to Waltz, the power of a theory is its ability to guide our attention to the important phenomena in the field, to enable us to ask the right questions, formulate fruitful hypotheses, stimulate and guide research, and provoke countertheories. The elegance of a theory is the ratio between its complexity and its range of explanation. An elegant theory is a simple one with a wide range. So a critique of theory is a questioning of the power and elegance of the whole theory in its capacity to guide the decision to focus on this or that item in the field and to control the formation of hypotheses for testing. Theory, therefore, orients research and facilitates understanding.
> (Hamerton-Kelly, 1994, p. 2)

And how, precisely, should theory orientate our research in the present time? If we are seeking an appropriate theory of interpretation for our age, we have to ask: what are the relevant and pressing features of our own culture which impinge on us, here and now? Elsewhere, Hamerton-Kelly declares the orienting significance of 'the hermeneutic of the Cross':

> I believe that the overriding fact of our time is violence; therefore a theory that attempts to make sense out of violence is more likely to orient us to the points in the field that are salient for our time . . . Therefore, there is a congruence between our times, our texts, and our tradition

that makes for a powerful interpretive constellation and vindicates my choice of the theory for a new initiative in the field.

(Hamerton-Kelly, 1992, p. 5)

Having said all of this, Girard himself is capable of disavowing the theoretical status of his work: 'Sensational and bizarre as it seems at first, the "theory" of mythology and ritual that I propose is not really a theory at all. It is a correction of persecutory distortions' (Girard, 1987c, p. 114). He will also refer more modestly to his 'insight' and 'thesis', as for example in the interview with *Diacritics* (1978). Here, Girard seeks to reassure those who fear in him a touch of megalomania, that he does not consider his insight as truly personal. Rather it is something 'in the air'. 'I view this insight as a minor part of that complete disintegration of sacrificial protections it is our misfortune and privilege to witness.' Responding to the question of how he is justified in asserting his theory in the absence of proper historical information, he suggests it is the qualitative accumulation of evidence which is compelling, rather than any theoretical refinement:

> I am not trying to make up that missing historical information through some fanciful story. I say that the aspects of religious forms dismissed as nonsensical by a still narrowly differential ethnology could be traces of a mimetic destructuration or crisis plus mimetic restructuration through unanimous victimage. If you confront that possibility with the reality of mythical and ritual forms you can quickly realize that, everywhere and always, everything does correspond to one or another of the innumerable combinations of distorted and also relatively undistorted representations that can be expected from such a process. My thesis is based entirely on structural inferences and it becomes compelling through the sheer number and variety of examples that can be exhibited.
>
> (Girard, 1978, p. 207)

So it is probable that the drive to establish the theoretical credentials of mimetic theory should not be over-indulged.

2. Mimetic Theory and Philosophy

Discussions about the 'scientific' status of Girard's theory have, on the whole, produced more heat than light. Critics will speak of Girard's discovery as a revisable hypothesis of science, or a revealed truth of theology, or some combination of the two. The other possibility is to situate Girard in the context of the *aftermath of modernity* – what Jean-Marie Domenach calls a 'voyage to the end of the sciences of man':

> The more I return to the work of René Girard, the more his 'hypothesis', as he calls it, appears to me as the heroic apogee of modern rationality: a voyage to the end of the sciences of man which, having reached the edge of the abyss of nihilism, do an amazing about-face that leads them back in a blazing journey to the very domain they believed they had left forever: that of the Word of God.
>
> (Dumouchel, 1988, p. 159)

It is a reversal by which 'reason, having completed its ravages' resorts to the Christian hypothesis which 'will give us at once meaning and hope, the one that will reunite intellect and love, the one that permits us to be, in a single motion, scientists and believers. Here we have a magnificent and unforeseen gift – too good, perhaps, to be accepted without caution and misgivings' (p. 153):

> However, if Girard restitutes the unity between our culture and our religion, if he places the Christian West back in the centre of the world, it is not at all through a triumphant operation of restoration; it is rather through a *revision*, in conformity with the best tradition of a West which never ceases reworking its myths and thereby finds itself alone able to give meaning. Self-destruction engenders self-affirmation; Girard appears at the outer limit of Lévi-Strauss's nihilism. Thus from a well-trod digging site the archaeologist of the eleventh hour unearths the decisive tablet (p. 152).

Nevertheless, Domenach is uncomfortable with Girard's ambiguity between a scientific and a philosophical position, since he occupies both but does not accept the burdens of either. In particular, assessing exactly the role that revelation plays in Girard's scheme is not an easy task; he is adamant that only a factor external to the cultures erected on the sacrificial mechanism – a divine factor – can expose that mechanism. What demystifies these cultures is not science, but the Christian *logos*. Not surprisingly, scientific collaborators with Girard, however sympathetic, will be unsure what to do with this kind of assertion.

One specific link with 'postmodern' philosophy should be noted. While at Johns Hopkins University in 1966, Girard was one of the organisers of a symposium entitled 'The Languages of Criticism and the Sciences of Man'. With Roland Barthes, Jacques Derrida, Jacques Lacan and other important critical theorists in attendance, the symposium was significant for bringing these new philosophical currents into the American academic scene. It also marked the beginning of Girard's engagement with the thought of Derrida. In his essay entitled 'Plato's Pharmacy', Derrida uses Plato's notion of the *pharmakon*, which means both 'remedy' and 'poison', to explore the ambiguity of writing; this essay is influential on Girard's development of the scapegoat thesis (*Violence and the Sacred*, pp. 295–7). The similarities between Derrida and Girard are explored at length in Andrew McKenna's *Violence and Difference* (McKenna, 1992), with the crucial observation that Girard's understanding of victimisation goes beyond textuality and engages with actuality.

More generally, we have seen in the course of this study that Girard has busied himself with a close reading of Hegel, Nietzsche and other philosophers, particularly from the French existentialist tradition. A meeting of the *Colloquium on Violence and Religion* in 2001 took 'Girard and Philosophy' as its theme, with contributions from Charles Taylor and Gianni Vattimo, while at a previous Colloquium, Paul Ricœur expressed his indebtedness to Girard's insights. The concern expressed by Domenach, that Girard occupies the position of a philosopher without accepting the philosopher's burdens, is a little unfair (one might sardonically ask, precisely what *are* the burdens and tasks of a philosopher nowadays?). In any case, although Girard does not claim to be a philosopher, he is nevertheless someone who has engaged positively with philosophical traditions and, in turn, a number of major philosophers have been appreciatively critical of René Girard's work.

There is a particular charge brought against Girard which should be mentioned, that his is a 'totalising' or even 'totalitarian' theory. As has been noted, he is a 'hedgehog thinker', who sees one thing or a small cluster of related things. Does this not make mimetic theory yet another 'grand narrative' of the oppressive kind associated with modernity? Once again, Jean-Marie Domenach expresses misgivings:

> If I voice an objection, is it to avoid succumbing to the seductiveness of an audacity that would return Christ on the cross to the centre of the world? It seems to me it is out of fear of meeting up again with some demons I thought I had exorcized: the claim to close off in a global explanation, the myth of a social transparency finally realized, the dream of a City that the Spirit would penetrate and dedicate to the Good. In short, a desire to know that does not know its limits and claims suddenly to illuminate all history, past, present and yet to come, like a pyrotechnics expert igniting a Catherine wheel. The tragic, in my view, will continue its dialogue with certitude. For there will subsist until the end a share of night that is not the reverse side of day, but the place for the propagation of light.
>
> (Dumouchel, 1988, p. 159)

In responding to such concerns, we would need to ask how far they represent a sincere and entirely laudable reservation about all-encompassing theoretical systems, which can indeed oppress and exclude – and how far they are symptoms of 'holophobia', a term used by Terry Eagleton (1996) to describe an attitude of excessive caution which paralyses all attempts at understanding and therefore at emancipatory action. Eagleton is thinking specifically of those aspects of postmodernism which betray a failure of intellectual nerve in the light of the collapse of socialism. He urges that 'the left, now more than ever, has need of strong ethical and even anthropological foundations' (1996, p. 134), a judgement strikingly similar to Girard's own protest against postmodernism. Eagleton's more recent book, *After Theory* (2003), in which he laments the increasing trivialisation and lack of ambition to be found in cultural theory, is an even more explicit exhortation to radical grand theorising:

> At just the point that we have begun to think small, history has begun to act big. . . . The inescapable

conclusion is that cultural theory must start thinking ambitiously once again – not so that it can hand the West its legitimation, but so that it can seek to make sense of the grand narratives in which it is now embroiled.

(Eagleton, 2003, pp. 72–3)

Girard recognises that attempts to develop a universal explanation of religions are now widely frowned upon, although from about 1860 until the middle of the twentieth century such an explanation was a kind of 'holy grail' for anthropologists. This search has come to be so widely discredited because too often it was conducted by researchers with little sympathy for religious belief, who were incapable of moving out of a Western scientific mentality. Nevertheless, Girard insists that the maturity of a science will be enhanced by its ability to acknowledge its cultural contextuality, and also to answer large and fundamental questions, especially when the discipline itself suffers from a lack of overall coherence:

> This is the greatness of our scientific tradition: that it never ceases to question its own premises in an effort to achieve greater objectivity. Even if this effort never proves entirely successful, it cannot be declared a failure, even in the social sciences. I think that anthropology should enjoy the same freedom to follow potentially productive intuitions as the natural sciences have always enjoyed. Anthropologists should disregard the puritan nihilism of our time and feel uninhibited about global interpretations, even if they are framed, as they cannot fail to be, in a context that reflects our own intellectual and spiritual tradition.
>
> (Girard, 1987c, p. 111)

3. The Anthropology of the Scapegoat

The passage quoted above, about Girard's method in spite of the lack of historical evidence for social origins, is a response to Claude Lévi-Strauss' judgement that the origins of symbolic thought, while a meaningful problem, cannot be solved. Girard recounts in *L'Envers du Mythe* (2001, pp. 154–167) the great enthusiasm with which he read Lévi-Strauss during the 1960s, especially when he was beginning to think about the theme of rivalrous twins. Lévi-Strauss' structuralism is to a large extent responsible for the contemporary rehabilitation of myth as a distinctive form of 'wild thinking' which eludes scientific rationality. Nevertheless, it is structuralism's inability to relate its insights to the question of origins and to actual victims that makes for the difference between his approach and Girard's.

In Chapter 9 of *Violence and the Sacred*, Girard enters into a fairly technical discussion of marriage laws and patterns of kinship according to Lévi-Strauss, with a view to highlighting what he sees as the main deficiencies of the structuralist method. Chapter 4 of *Things Hidden*, 'Myth: The Invisibility of the Founding Murder' is a close analysis of Lévi-Strauss' comparison (in *Totemism*) of two myths which seem to share a common theme of totemistic clan culture arising from the expulsion of gods. Lévi-Strauss traces in both myths a 'radical elimination' of particular elements, which allows a system of distinctions and cultural order to come into being. However, for Lévi-Strauss, the expulsion is a purely fictive representation of a cultural development. Because he is restricted to the linguistic dimension of the myth, he is unable to recognise that it is rooted in real events. This same limitation causes Lévi-Strauss to separate myth from ritual, and to devalue the latter (for Girard, of course, myth and ritual are closely related, both being grounded in the scapegoat mechanism).

Girard acknowledges that Lévi-Strauss' insights are certainly better than what has gone before, and have indeed helped mimetic theory to advance one vital stage further. Nevertheless, the weakness of his structuralism is that 'as with all myths before his, he has done nothing but invent a new jargon in which to transfigure the representation of lynching' (p. 124). Commenting on the disturbing account of the ritual marriage of cross-cousins among the Tsimshian people, in which 'stones are thrown and many heads battered', Girard notes wryly: 'It is easy to imagine a twentieth-century Cervantes or Molière planting in the midst of those flying stones a devotee of the self-referential text in order to prove to him that some metaphors are more striking than others' (1977, p. 248). Structuralism 'is itself locked into the structure, a prisoner of the synchronic' (1977, p. 242); a deficient mode of thought 'that circles around the problem of origins without ever coming to grips with it – that in fact foregoes the opportunity to come to grips with it in favor of pure formalism' (1977, p. 235).

Obviously, if one has decided, on structuralist or other grounds,

that a search for origins such as Girard undertakes is doomed to failure, then there is no further conversation to be had. A more useful
critique will come from thinkers who are trying to construct a
theory of origins on a similarly grand scale, and who are therefore
able to identify fruitful areas of disagreement and convergence. A
distinctive contribution to be mentioned here is that of a pupil of
Girard's, Eric Gans, at the University of California, whose own
development of 'Generative Anthropology' or 'GA' is probably the
most extensive engagement with the anthropological and scientific
ramifications of mimetic theory. Gans focuses upon the fascinated
attitude towards the corpse of the sacred victim, to offer his own
version of an originary hypothesis. For Gans, human language
begins as an aborted gesture of appropriation, representing – and
thereby renouncing as sacred – an object of potential mimetic
rivalry. Language defers potential conflict by permitting each to
possess the sign of the unpossessable object of desire – the deferral
of violence through representation. 'The originary hypothesis
provides the basis for rethinking every aspect of the human, from
language to art, from religion to political organization.'

A special issue of *Anthropoetics* (the electronic journal of
Generative Anthropology) acknowledges its debt to Girard's thought
(Gans, 1996). It contains an interview with Girard, and Gans' own
summary of how he sees the relationship between the two modes of
thinking. GA brings together mimetic theory and deconstruction,
mimesis and *différance*, in its characterisation of the human by the
deferral of violence through representation:

> In the Girardian scenario of 'hominization', the violence
> of mimetic rivalry is controlled anew by the murder of a
> scapegoat or emissary victim which (Girard would say,
> *who*) by becoming the first 'signifier' institutes a new
> means of founding intracultural differences. The victim
> 'signifies' by his transcendent power to focus violence, and
> thereby to end it. As he is perceived as the destroyer of the
> differences on which the self-reproductive activities of life
> depend, the communal energy normally devoted to these
> activities becomes absorbed in his killing. As a conse-
> quence, with his death, the victim is perceived as bestow-
> ing on us these differences and the activities that depend

on them, henceforth understood as dependent on his good will. The human order, as opposed to the animal order that preceded it, is made dependent on the sacred as defined by its own violence; we are the only species to which mimetic violence poses a greater threat than the extraspecific natural world. But human differences differ from animal differences precisely because they are formulated in *language*. This is the one aspect of mimesis that Derrida understands better than Girard. The advantage of the linguistic sign is expressed in the parable of the loaves and fishes that, like the word of God, may be multiplied indefinitely. If, as Girard claims, the original 'signifier' were a corpse, language would be an expensive affair indeed. The corpse of the victim becomes the foundation of human culture not as the first sign, but as the *referent* of the first sign.

(Gans, 1996, p. 1)

A similar attempt to take seriously the investigation of human origins is the conference on *Violent Origins* which brings together Girard, Walter Burkert and Jonathan Z. Smith, with three very different points of departure on the subject of religion (Hamerton-Kelly, 1987). Walter Burkert's *Homo Necans* was published in German in 1972, the same year as *Violence and the Sacred*; each offering a startling new account of religion based on ritual killing – though for Burkert it is the hunt, in which animals are killed for food, which is primary, not the killing of a human victim.

According to Burton Mack, these theories should be seen in terms of a struggle between a 'human sciences' approach to religion (which they represent), and a more traditional 'history and phenomenology of religion' position. All three thinkers promote an understanding of religion as a social phenomenon, using empirical approaches which draw on the human sciences, and without resorting to a mystique of 'the Sacred' to explain religion's attractiveness. They share a view that religion arises in relation to some human activity fundamental to social life, although they have very divergent views on what that activity is. The traditionalist objection is that this newer perspective cannot be said to account for everything that is meant by 'religion'. At issue here is the notion of the Sacred, which, for the earlier consensus, is irreducible. All other approaches are 'reductionist', in which case René Girard (and Burkert) fall firmly into the 'reductionist' camp. For these theorists:

> No longer does an epiphanic object of being focus the picture for the religious imagination, providing a center around which a Sacred Order is organized by means of a system of symbols. Instead an act (action, activity) has been noticed as a transaction of consequence, reflected on as patterned sequence, and cultivated in ritual as of prime importance.

(Mack, 1987, pp. 58–9)

Burton Mack suggests we should not underestimate the tremendous pressure that such a shift puts on our linguistic and cultural resources. He sees each of the authors presenting a 'scenario' or ritual script: that is, a description of a scene, action, agent and object, as well as an account of purpose. In each case, the scenario is heuristic (that is, a hypothetical scheme, rather than one that is formally being 'proved'), and also intentionally provocative. It reveals to us both the kind of interpretation being used, and the assumptions about human nature which are in play.

For both Girard and Burkert, 'the act of killing is definitional for human social being', though the central *impasse* between them is that for Burkert it is the prey, killed for food, who is the primary victim, while for Girard it is the human scapegoat. Each faces a similar challenge, however, when it comes to evidence: can the data adjudicate between them? Whatever supporting evidence Girard and Burkert may bring in from elsewhere, 'ritual sacrifice must serve as evidence for theories that seek to explain it . . . we must hope for lots of texts on the table' (Mack, 1987, p. 62).

Girard's paper to the seminar, 'Generative Scapegoating', distinguishes the different senses of the term 'scapegoat' and clarifies his own usage, and analyses three myths to illustrate his theory. In the discussion which follows, Smith takes issue with Girard's selectivity in choosing a version of an Amazonian myth (one of perhaps five) which has a 'dark', i.e. violent content, instead of the several hundred other versions of the same myth that do not. Girard does not see this as a problem, since the fruitfulness of his method lies in the juxtaposition of similar myths or 'chains' of myths, some of which will have more visible elements of violence than others. His strategy is to move from more transparent to less transparent myths, and in so doing to become ever more adept at discerning the traces of displacement.

It emerges from the discussion that Walter Burkert and René Girard offer 'maximalist' theories (and therefore make themselves vulnerable to criticism on a wide front), while Smith can be described as a 'minimalist', whose theory is the least adventurous of the three. While Smith's caution may in itself be admirable, we are still left with the problem of origins, one that no genuine science can evade if it is to make progress. What becomes evident from this encounter is that even among scholars who may be broadly sympathetic to a theory of this range and scope, the difficulty of establishing common terms of reference, vocabulary, methodology and so on, is immense. And given this lack of agreement, there is virtually no part of Girard's system that is not open to criticism.

A positive appraisal of mimetic theory will at least agree with Girard on two things. First, that the turn to the 'human sciences' approach to religion, and therefore the turning away from 'the Sacred' as the primary focus, in order to pay more attention to human social activity, is legitimate. Secondly, that to ask about the origin of religion is not only worthwhile but necessary, even if this leaves open the possibility of being linked with previous theories of origin which have been discredited. But beyond this, there will be many details that, for most critics, will require much further discussion.

4. Girard and Historical Christianity

We should address what seems to be one of the most glaring objections. The first two phases of the mimetic hypothesis – mimetic desire and the scapegoating mechanism – have at least an initial plausibility. But since in the third phase Girard goes on to claim that the scapegoat mechanism is fully unmasked in the New Testament, we have to ask why, in the course of the Church's history, so many events have occurred which follow the same pattern of collective persecution. How is it that, despite the fact that its most cherished texts stand in total opposition to persecutory myth, Christianity finds itself complicit in the coercion of heretics, Jews and witches?

The single, most telling counter-example to Girard's theory, in other words, is the bloodstained history of the Christian Church.

Strong forms of this objection have even maintained that the gospel stories themselves are, in their very structure, precisely the kind of persecution text which, on Girard's account, they are supposed to unveil and deconstruct. Burton Mack has framed precisely this serious objection to Girard's theory in his article in *Semeia* (Mack, 1985). Written as they are at a painful juncture in Jewish–Christian relations, their scapegoating of the Jewish people as the rejecters and killers of Christ is more than incidental, it is crucial to their theological structure.

Girard addresses the concern about Christianity's historical record in some detail in a chapter of *Things Hidden*, entitled 'The Sacrificial Reading and Historical Christianity' (pp. 224–62). Here and elsewhere he is at pains to disallow the charge of anti-Semitism in the gospels, precisely because the gospels make it clear that *everyone* was united against Jesus. The Jewish and Roman authorities joined the mob in complete harmony, while even the disciples, in fleeing and denying Jesus, succumbed to the universal mimeticism of the scapegoat. That later generations of Christians should corrupt these insights into an excuse for persecuting the Jews is not the fault of the evangelical text, and is even in a sense what we might be led to expect, if we recognise that the destabilising evangelical deconstruction of the violent sacred will engender situations of even greater persecution in the short term.

Girard maintains that the Gospel is total revelation without concealment, but that we can take it only gradually: an 'unrecognised revelation', in so far as invisible aspects of the text have become more perceptible in our current era. He asserts that 'nothing is clear-cut . . . In history, we are always between the gospel and myth.' Nevertheless, his historical thesis remains an audacious one, that the West's move away from scapegoating (such as it is), and towards a desacralised world which effortlessly sees through scapegoating and makes us instinctive partisans for the victim – this history is the product not of an Enlightenment rationality, banishing the darkness of religious superstition, but of the evangelical impulse itself. It is the Paraclete, the 'advocate for the defence', working subterraneously at the foundations of cultures, who has effected and continues to effect this stupendous change.

Here there is much work to be done, perhaps by way of 'archaeology' in Foucault's sense, if we are to validate this account of Christianity's role in Western culture. We have something like a version of Weber's thesis, though Dumouchel (1988, p. 20) suggests that our knowledge of how capitalism and the modern world came into being is still too tenuous to establish its validity. Girard's reversal of the accepted version of events at the dawn of modernity, which he sets out in the final chapter of *The Scapegoat*, 'History and the Paraclete', remains one of the most tantalising aspects of his theory:

> The scientific spirit cannot come first. It presupposes the renunciation of a former preference for the magical causality of persecution so well defined by the ethnologists. Instead of natural, distant and inaccessible causes, humanity has always preferred causes that are significant from a social perspective and which permit of corrective intervention – victims. In order to lead men to the patient exploration of natural causes, men must first be turned away from their victims. This can only be done by showing them that from now on persecutors 'hate without cause' and without any appreciable result. In order to achieve this miracle, not only among certain exceptional individuals as in Greece, but for entire populations, there is need of the extraordinary combination of intellectual, moral and religious factors found in the Gospel text.
>
> The invention of science is not the reason that there are no longer witch-hunts, but the fact that there are no longer witch-hunts is the reason that science has been invented. The scientific spirit, like the spirit of enterprise in an economy, is a by-product of the profound action of the Gospel text. The modern Western world has forgotten the revelation in favour of its by-products, making them weapons and instruments of power; and now the process has turned against it. Believing itself a liberator, it discovers its role as a persecutor.
>
> (Girard, 1986, pp. 204–5)

5. Girard's 'Gnosticism'

The charge of 'gnosticism' has been leveled at Girard from several quarters: the tag, to be sure, is profoundly unenlightening, but the misgivings it seeks to articulate must be addressed. Charles Davis feels constrained to reject Girard's hypothesis on account of its 'lack of humility' and its 'gnostic anthropology' by which 'human beings are regarded as incapable of making a society for themselves. They are locked into a mutually destructive violence from which they cannot extricate themselves' (Davis, 1989, p. 321). Jean-Marie Domenach once again:

> The great difficulty one encounters in conceiving of an ethics and a politics in the Girardian perspective stems, I think, from being torn between a constraining nature and a remote God – a gulf which can be filled by intellect but not by action. The gnostic aspect of Girard's thought, so convincing and at times so intoxicating, thus comes at the price of the impossibility of any historical thought or practice, whether personal or collective, in the middle of such a distance.
>
> (Dumouchel, 1988, p. 155)

The label 'gnostic' is frankly too imprecise to be very helpful. We have seen in the last chapter that Girard's is a very 'Johannine' Christianity, and this might perhaps explain the 'quasi-gnostic' tenor of some of his statements. A more pertinent objection is that of the lack of a discernible political practice in Girard's scheme. This is similar to that put forward by John Milbank (*Theology and Social Theory*, 1990), who draws attention to the absence in Girard's theory of a positive alternative to sacred violence, a 'counter-sacrificial practice'.

Is it the case that Girard's theory is paralysing in this way? Mimetic theory seems to be extremely forceful as an explanation of what happens to societies which are collapsing into crisis, but less helpful in envisaging positive societies of conviviality. Girard's insistence on the destructive potential of mimetic desire leads him to a radical questioning of human autonomy, as we have seen, and also to assert that ideologies of liberation are self-defeating:

> The more people think they are realizing the Utopias dreamed up by their desire – in other words, the more they embrace ideologies of liberation – the more they will in fact be working to reinforce the competitive world that

is stifling them . . . All modern thought is falsified by a
mystique of transgression, which it falls back into even
when it is trying to escape.

(Girard, 1987a, p. 287)

A similar impression is left from the meeting of Girard and a number of Latin American liberation theologians in Brazil in 1990
(Assmann, 1991), where those theologians present challenge Girard
about his pessimism as to the possibility of genuine solidarity in
human communities (a crucial theme, obviously, for liberation
theology). Perhaps one should say that this dimension of Girard's
thought is open to further development. The criticisms recounted
above express misgivings about what is perceived to be Girard's
pessimistic analysis of society. It is a huge distortion of his thinking,
however, to say that humanity is helpless and incapable of emancipatory action. What is at issue is not the impossibility of progress, but
the difficulty and precariousness of any movement away from
mimetic enslavement. Loose accusations of 'gnosticism' do not help:
fundamental Christian doctrines such as the goodness of creation
and free will are firmly in place in Girard's system, even if he does
not stress them. But the gauntlet has been thrown down by too
many critics not to be taken seriously, and here is a particular challenge for political theorists who wish to work with mimetic theory,
to refute the unfair label of 'reactionary'.

6. Girard and the Theologians
Girard has on a number of occasions expressed his indebtedness to
Raymund Schwager, the Swiss Jesuit who has been one of his
foremost theological commentators, even going so far as to suggest
that Schwager is one of the few commentators not to have misrep-
resented him (Assmann, 1991). Schwager has made extensive use
of the mimetic theory, especially in his construction of a 'dramatic
theology', while Girard's appreciation of 'sacrifice' has developed
under Schwager's influence. In his three principal works, Schwager
has used Girardian anthropology to look at the theme of (God's)
violence in the Bible in *Must there be Scapegoats?* (1987), to lay the
basis for a systematic soteriology (articles collected together in *Der
wunderbare Tausch*, 1986), and to construct a dramatic interpretation

of the ministry, death and resurrection of Jesus in *Jesus and the Drama of Salvation* (2001).

His conclusion in *Must there be Scapegoats?* concurs with Girard's, that in the Bible, God is progressively revealed as loving, non-violent and on the side of innocent victims. Schwager establishes on this foundation a theory of redemption: Jesus' response of non-vengeance delivers men from the evil and hatred from which they cannot free themselves. Very much to the fore in Schwager's account is the need to reinterpret concepts such as the 'wrath of God' and 'sacrifice' so that they do not impute violence to God. Schwager's readings of soteriological themes are collected together in *Der wunderbare Tausch*, while in *Jesus and the Drama of Salvation*, as we have seen, he presents a 'dramatic' understanding of Jesus' role in five acts.

His dramatic soteriology represents the most thorough application of René Girard's concept of the scapegoat mechanism to christological questions. In a symposium on 'dramatic soteriology' in 1991, Schwager responds to the question, 'is it necessary for a dramatic doctrine of redemption in the long run to have regard to the scapegoat theory?' He insists that although new theological currents, such as political, liberation, feminist and ecological theologies, all practise theology from the perspective of the victim, none offer 'a thoroughly elaborated (anthropological, cultural, social, religious-scientific and theological) theory' which would focus on the victim. 'Theology needs a religious theory of the victim that covers all fields of human science', such as that offered by René Girard (Niewiadomski and Palaver, 1992, pp. 354–5).

On another occasion, Girard compares his own work in *Things Hidden* with the conclusions of *Must there be Scapegoats?*, which came out at the same time. He congratulates Schwager for his boldness in reclaiming the language and conceptuality of sacrifice at a point when he himself was hesitant, for apologetic reasons, to blur what he saw as the crucial difference between the Christian revelation and other religions:

> I believed that the overriding significance of the mimetic theory had to be in directing all apologetic efforts against religious relativism. It was to expose its weaknesses. I wanted nothing other than to make even more precise the clarity of this position, which pressed upon me almost like

a proof . . . For this reason I had for a long time considered this usage [Christian sacrifice] to be degenerate.
(Niewiadomski and Palaver, 1995, p. 24)

An important text which helped Girard to a more nuanced understanding of sacrifice is the dispute before Solomon of the two
women concerning the rightful ownership of a baby. Here are the
two very different meanings of the word: the 'blood' sacrifice, proposed by Solomon, of slicing the infant in two (which the false
mother is only too ready to accept); and the genuine sacrifice,
through love, on the part of the baby's true mother, as she is prepared
to give up the child. It is worth pointing out Girard's admission in
an interview (Adams, 1993), that in *Things Hidden* he had 'scapegoated' the letter to the Hebrews, and also the word 'sacrifice',
assuming it should have a constant meaning. 'In fact, the changes in
its meaning constitute the religious history of mankind.'

A specific theological critique of Girard and Schwager, from the
Swiss theologian, Hans Urs von Balthasar, is significant for this discussion. His version of dramatic theology (contained in a substantial
multi-volume work called the *Theodrama*) is in part a model for
Raymund Schwager's own dramatic theological synthesis. Balthasar
even considers the theological resonances of the statue scene in *The
Winter's Tale,* as discussed by Girard above. In volume IV of the
Theodrama ('The Action'), Balthasar sets out his understanding of
soteriology, or theory of salvation. He stresses that the notion of
solidarity as the key to understanding the way Jesus saves human
beings is insufficient. There has also to be some understanding of
Christ's *substitution* for us, if we are to be faithful to the biblical
witness concerning our salvation.

He judges the theory of René Girard, which combines these two
approaches, to be 'surely the most dramatic project to be undertaken today in the field of soteriology and in theology generally'
(Balthasar, 1994, p. 299). Balthasar is broadly sympathetic to the
approach of Girard and Schwager, but offers a number of criticisms.
He concurs with Girard's reversal of Nietzsche's antithesis, 'the
Crucified versus Dionysus', though he also claims that Girard has
'distorted' Anselm's theory of sacrifice. He also questions Girard's
insistent use of the terminology of 'power' and 'violence' to the
neglect of 'justice' (especially the justice of God, never acknow-

ledged as primary by Girard), before voicing his most far-reaching misgivings:

> The dramatic tension between the world and God is so overstretched that the link breaks, rendering impossible a drama that involves the two sides. This is clear from the fact that the self-concealing 'mechanism' eliminates all freedom on man's part. Girard maintains a complete hiatus between naturalism and theology; they are not even linked by an ethics . . . This raises a question that is crucial in the present context: what takes place on the Cross, according to this theory, if the transferral of the world's guilt to Jesus is only a psychological unloading (as it was in all ritual sacrifice), and if – on the other hand – the power-less Father–God demands nothing in the nature of an 'atoning sacrifice'?
>
> (Balthasar, 1994, pp. 309–10)

For Balthasar, the dramatic theology of Schwager and Girard fails *as drama*. It overemphasises the social dynamic of the Crucifixion and underplays its significance as an event between the Father and the Son. Both Girard and Schwager concentrate on the human attitude to the Crucified, and say nothing of God's attitude. Yet Isaiah 53:6 presents us 'inescapably' with a God who either wills the burdening of the Servant or allows it, and their analysis fails to arrive at the real problem, namely the relationship between God's justice and his power (p. 312).

A fairly substantial gulf between these authors remains, therefore: Balthasar insists upon attributing some level of complicity, therefore violence, to God in the crucifixion (and in the suffering of the Servant in Second Isaiah). In short, he wishes to hold onto God's 'wrath' in terms of his ability to exact retribution. Schwager and Girard, for all that their dramatic theology bears similarities to Balthasar's, are unable to follow him on this point. Nevertheless, there is much in Balthasar's critique which is of value, namely his judicious recognition of Girard's original approach, and of the possibility of resolving particular difficulties in the theology of atonement.

The citation of Anselm is also interesting. Balthasar has contributed to the contemporary reappraisal of Anselm's argument, and therefore his 'rehabilitation' from being associated with crude notions of penal substitution. In fact there now appear to be striking similarities between Anselm and Girard, as each can be seen as attempting to systematise an intuition about how the Gospel message is relevant for their own time. Whether mimetic theory can justly be described as 'faith seeking understanding' would be another discussion. Certainly, Girard's impact on theology has been considerable, as theologians recognise in his work a new way of conceiving of the doctrine of the atonement, and in particular a fresh contribution to Christianity's theological understanding of sacrifice.

7. Feminist Critiques of Mimetic Theory

Susan Nowak (1994) offers an overview of Girard's reception by feminist critics, as well as her own critique. There have been reservations on the part of feminist and Freudian critics – Toril Moi (1982), Luce Irigaray (1986), Sarah Kofman (1987) and Nancy Jay (1992) – who take issue with Girard's treatment of narcissism in *Things Hidden*, and more generally judge Girard's concentration on almost exclusively male configurations of desire and violence to be an indicator of his misogyny. Part of the evidence for this is that most of his examples of victimhood are male, as are nearly all the authors he cites. This particular charge is, as Girard has pointed out, bizarre and unfair, though it does highlight the wider question of how far his account of sacrificial violence coheres with similar feminist investigations into the nature of violence against women.

Here, more than ever, it is important not to separate Girard's victimary hypothesis from the account of mimetic desire. Girard is adamant that desire is mimetic for both sexes. Once again, his principal objection is against Freud, who in his theory of narcissism held to a view of two types of sexual desire, each of which was gender-specific. On this question, Girard holds out for equality between men and women, a position which will be inimical to anyone who wishes to highlight allegedly essential differences between them.

A different matter is whether Girard's theory can yield an adequate account of misogynist violence and oppression, since in most cultures there is anything but equality on this score. This is acknowledged by Girard and certainly compatible with his thesis. Scapegoats are chosen because of their vulnerability, and so the physical weakness of women compared to men makes them more likely candidates. This should not be overstated: Martha Reineke (1990) finds mimetic theory immensely helpful for discussion of the European witch-craze, while by contrast Anne L. Barstow contends that few of Girard's scapegoat criteria apply to the witch-trials, apart from the marginality of the victims. Executions of witches were not communal events which produced a sacral reconciliation, but simply brutal 'rituals of nullity, dead ends' (Barstow, 1995, pp. 153–4). This is a salutary reminder that not every victim is a 'scapegoat' in the technical sense that Girard intends.

Girard's theory does, however, cast an unsettling light on the discussion of allegedly matriarchal or matrifocal ancient civilisations. These cultures, supposedly more egalitarian and less violent than patriarchal ones, would be typified by the prevalence of female deities. A Girardian reading would, of course, insist that evidence of more goddesses simply means that more women were sacrificed in these cultures, not fewer.

Jennifer L. Rike (1996) questions whether the rush of feminists to condemn Girard for androcentrism might indicate their reluctance to confront the issue of violence in women as well as men. This is clearly a dangerous evasion, since the reality of women's internalising the violence perpetrated against them is a crucial issue. The specific charges they make against Girard, that he universalises conceptions of humanity, violence and religion which are Eurocentric and androcentric, may well have some degree of truth (though Girard would be prepared to defend this universalisation). Rike prefers to look for positive ways in which mimetic theory can and should be taken up by feminism, as a way out of its current identity crisis. She suggests that Girard's conception of acquisitive mimesis needs to be complemented by object relations theory, to enable feminist reconstructions of selfhood which are true to the ambiguity of women's experience (the scapegoat is itself an ambiguous phenomenon). Girard's insistence on the identity of the cognitive and psychical structures of men and women is valid, but women's modes of embodiment, and their social, economic and political positioning, are clearly different. As yet, the theoretical apparatus for comprehending this identity and this difference together is still lacking, and feminism cannot afford to ignore Girard's insights.

CHAPTER 5

The Future of Mimetic Theory

In one sense, a chapter entitled 'The Future of Mimetic Theory' writes itself. Girard is adamant that the disabling of the scapegoat mechanism is a two-edged sword. Of course it is good news that we are now aware of how innocent people are frequently victimised in order to maintain social stability. As this awareness spreads, so scapegoating becomes – indeed, has become – less credible and less effective.

But what happens, then, to social stability, if communities no longer have recourse to this time-honoured way of channelling violence? We recall that humanity lacks the instinctual brakes on aggression that prevent animals from tearing themselves apart. And this period of vulnerability, when we find ourselves deprived of a key defence against limitless violence, coincides with an era when the human race has the technology to destroy itself completely. All Girard's key texts were written under the shadow of the Cold War, when the appropriately named Mutually Assured Destruction (MAD) was the orthodox doctrine for 'peaceful' cohabitation on earth. The implications of this situation were not lost on Girard. He is convinced of the power and success of the Gospel message in transforming the world and ridding it of scapegoat ideology; but what humankind does with this knowledge is still an open question.

And in our age, with the technology we have at our disposal, this is nothing less than the choice specified in Deuteronomy 30:19: 'I set before you this day, life and good, death and evil. Choose good, that you may live!' Either we will – all of us – undertake the kind of renunciation and non-violent love which is at the heart of the Gospel message; or we will carry on as normal, and we will die, because our inoculations against overwhelming violence no longer work. Hence the irony of reflecting upon the 'future' of mimetic theory, because of the bleak prospect that Girard's theory will turn out to be true but there may be no one around to verify it.

In a less apocalyptic sense, the future of mimetic theory lies with a body called the *Colloquium on Violence and Religion* (COV&R), which gathers together scholars, mainly from USA and Europe, who have been gripped with Girard's ideas and who wish 'to explore, criticise, and develop the mimetic model of the relationship between violence and religion in the genesis and maintenance of culture'. The Colloquium has been meeting since 1990, with René Girard as its honorary president, and produces a journal, *Contagion*. A survey of COV&R's activities would give some indication of where its members see the priorities for mimetic theory; such a survey is easily done by visiting COV&R's website, however, and what would be more useful here is to pick out a few directions and tendencies which seem to me pertinent.

We must return to questions of just how 'theoretical' the mimetic insight is intended to be. In the Introduction, the dilemma was posed as to whether Girard's mimetic theory should be thought of as a floodlight which illuminates everything, or as a collection of tastefully arranged spotlights, picking out local details. One of the idiosyncrasies of COV&R's *raison d'être*, as stated above, is that both options seem to be possible. Some members hold that mimetic theory is an anthropological discovery of immense importance, and they work to establish its scientific and theoretical credentials; others agree about its importance but are keen to resist any overt attempt towards its 'systematisation'. Then there are others, including possibly René Girard himself, who seem to manage to hold both views at the same time.

We have looked at Robert Hamerton-Kelly's discussion of Girard's work in terms of a responsible framing of theories and hypotheses in science. The contribution of Eric Gans has also been examined: his originary hypothesis first appears in *The Origin of Language* (Gans, 1981), while the electronic journal, *Anthropoetics* (together with its wonderfully entitled weekly column, *Chronicles of Love and Resentment*) is dedicated to the development of Generative Anthropology, both for its intrinsic importance and as a framework for literary and cultural analysis. For Gans, the discovery of the sign as an aborted gesture of appropriation that becomes a representation, is the discovery that our capacity for mimesis, the basis for our rivalrous sharing of desire, can also become the basis for the peaceful sharing of significance. It is the world of signs that is the source of our understanding of the world of transcendence. Gans does not find this incompatible with a religious perspective, according to which the existence of human language, incommensurable with animal signal-systems and inexplicable by positive science, is only possible as a divine gift, though he regards this question as indecidable. Gans pays fulsome tribute to Girard's inspiration for his own project:

> ... above all in the grandeur of his intellectual ambition and in his unshakeable confidence in the superiority of real thinking to fashionable thought-play. As the one true anthropologist, Girard is living proof that the cultural self-reflection of the Humanities offers a better model for thinking the human than the positivism of the social sciences. No one could serve as a better mimetic model for us all.
>
> (Gans, 1996, p. 2)

Another example of a sustained attempt to establish a firm theoretical foundation for mimetic insight would be the interdisciplinary Research Group, based at the University of Innsbruck, working on 'Religion – Violence – Communication – World Order'. Here, Raymund Schwager and a number of colleagues from theology and other faculties have established a research programme, using the framework of Imre Lakatos, which 'seeks a reconciliation between alternative views as to the falsification of scientific theories'. The group has elaborated general hypotheses, hard core hypotheses and auxiliary hypotheses, among which the mimetic insights of René Girard are prominent.

I mention these initiatives, not to entangle us once again in technical discussion, but to illustrate some directions that mimetic theory has taken. It is highly probable that this work is exciting and will prove to be extremely fruitful. On the other hand, there are those who are interested primarily in René Girard's discoveries as a *hermeneutic* – a way of reading texts of all sorts with a view to our being 'converted' by what we read. Mimetic theory is the 'destroyer of systems', it calls us to keep on reading and allow oneself to be drawn into an ever more authentic 'living in truth'. Here, it is the pastoral implications of Girard's theory which are primary, and which impress themselves on those working directly in pastoral ministries, conflict resolution, spirituality, justice and peace, and so on.

The work of Gil Bailie, in the United States, and James Alison, an English theologian, each exemplify this option. Bailie's *Violence Unveiled: Humanity at the Crossroads* (1995) is a work of urgent cultural criticism as prophetic theology. The urgency comes from the 'apocalyptic' crisis of social breakdown and violence in contemporary USA, which he analyses through a Girardian lens. Bailie draws on literature, film, newspapers, and a dizzying portfolio of cultural indicators as well as the Bible; much of the power of his writing comes from this gift of effective and startling juxtaposition. If we recall from Chapter 2 that mimetic theory is understood as a moving between different texts which have different degrees of revelatory power – between 'myth', 'literature' and 'criticism' – then Bailie's work would be an impressive example of this criticism.

James Alison speaks openly of an immense personal and intellectual debt to Girard, prominent in all his own writings. Among these are *The Joy of Being Wrong*, a recasting of the doctrine of original sin using mimetic theory (the topic of Alison's doctoral thesis, completed in Brazil); *Raising Abel*, which deals with eschatology; and a number of more popular books, which, while certainly theologically informed, have a more informal and personal style. The chapters in *Faith Beyond Resentment: Fragments Catholic and Gay* (2001) and *On Being Liked* (2003) are based for the most part on talks to various groups, in academic and non-academic settings, or are sustained meditations on particular passages from Scripture.

Alison sees in Girard's insights the possibility of creatively reworking Christian themes such as creation and salvation, eschatology, natural law, sin and forgiveness, and religious integrity, in a way that is Catholic and liberating. But there is only a minimal 'systematisation' of these doctrines, since Alison is more concerned about how we come to 'inhabit' a particular story, at base the story of a love so surprising and gratuitous that he and we can only share our wonder and our struggle to make sense of it. This, he suggests, is theology which 'stutters'. In other words, Alison's deliberately tentative approach sounds much more like the struggle towards 'novelistic truth' that is the *alpha* and *omega* of Girard's own journey, than an extensive dogmatic synthesis. By implication, a conversion/resurrection experience cannot be part of a 'system'.

I want immediately to defuse the apparent contradiction that I have just set up between these two approaches – the one seeking to establish the mimetic theory very firmly on sound and lasting theoretical foundations, the other concerned simply to keep reading, as it were, with eyes being ever more opened by conversion. Both are options within the general remit of COV&R, to 'explore, criticise and develop the mimetic model', and both are important. What I would propose is that these two strategies make sense in terms of two different audiences and two different tasks. The work of Bailie and Alison will be read for the most part by people who are already engaged with the Christian tradition, either as committed believers or as people who feel themselves to have a problematic relation to it (although Alison expresses the hope that the implications of his writing go well beyond the specific interests of any particular marginal group). These are the people who will, by and large, have an initial interest in seeing how the central narratives of the Christian faith can be creatively retold.

Both the proponents of Generative Anthropology and the Innsbruck Research Group have a different, explicitly interdisciplinary focus, in so far as they address hugely urgent social and political issues *ad extra*, as it were. Here the question is not primarily that of reconfiguring the narratives of Christianity. Rather, the task is to assist in making sense of disturbing phenomena, for which adequate tools of understanding are not yet to hand. With the Research Group in particular, realities such as globalisation, religious-inspired violence and so on, are of course the burning issues of the day, though what is especially perplexing is the 'return of religion' which has taken many people by surprise, and which requires new paradigms of thinking.

From this it appears that the specific value and contribution of mimetic theory, given institutional form in a group like COV&R, is twofold. It can enable *a structured and responsible reflection upon religion in the contemporary world*, and it can offer *a way of reading stories so that faith, hope and love may be challenged, confirmed, nourished, or even called into being.*

The Return of Religion

At the beginning of the discussion in *Things Hidden*, as Girard is introducing his hypothesis, he makes some intriguing remarks:

Science is the distinctive achievement of the modern mind. In each incontestable scientific conquest, the same process is repeated: what had been an age-old, dark and formidable mystery is transformed into an enigma. There is no enigma, however complex, that cannot finally be solved. For centuries religion has been declining in the West and its disappearance is now a global phenomenon. As religion recedes and allows us to consider it in perspective, what was once an insoluble mystery, guarded by formidable taboos, begins to looks more and more like a problem to be solved.

(Girard, 1987a, p. 3)

Leaving aside Girard's apparently strident confidence in the power of science, it is clear that his remarks about the universal decline of religion – a worldwide ebbing of the 'sea of faith' – no longer carry the conviction they may have done twenty-five years ago. The current orthodoxy among sociologists of religion is that theories of secularisation have failed as an explanatory tool, most especially where they extrapolate from the West's experience and predict increasing secularisation on a global scale. Other sociologists will argue to the contrary that Europe is to be regarded as an 'exceptional case', with no indication that the rest of the world will follow the patterns of change that have occurred there. Even in Europe, what we are seeing is a displacement and relocation of religious forms, the emergence of 'intermediate transcendencies', rather than a disappearance of the sacred as such.

In spite of what the comments of Girard might suggest, at no point is mimetic theory dependent upon a theory of secularisation, though perhaps the new consensus will change the way mimetic theory is tested and developed. More recently (in *Quand ces choses commenceront*), Girard has explicitly distanced himself from Marcel Gauchet's claim (1997) that Christianity has brought about the end of religion in the world. Rather, he suggests, our current humanism will be perceived as merely a short interval between two forms of religion.

For this reason, mimetic theory, which gives a plausible account of why religion might be expected to persist in the world, is in some ways well placed to fill the vacuum left by theories of secularisation.

And while it is essential that the 'return of religion' is not reduced and distorted into concerns, however legitimate, about religious extremism and 'fundamentalist' violence, there is clearly a contribution to be made here. A collection of 'case studies' entitled *Violence and the Sacred in the Modern World* (1992) has been edited by Mark Juergensmeyer, a former student of Girard's and a theorist of religious violence. This volume looks at a number of contemporary conflicts in which religious belief is at least a major component of the tension, and investigates which of these may be illuminated by mimetic theory.

It is in the shadow of 11 September, of course, that much of the most anguished reflection about sacred violence has taken place. Very soon after the atrocity occurred, a number of typical positions could be discerned. For example, Richard Dawkins, a noted secularist thinker, decried in a newspaper article the most dangerous weapon of all, namely religion: this weapon had been honed over millennia, and was now proving as destructive as ever. In other words, the problem lay with those who espoused religious belief as such, and who therefore found themselves the enemies of enlightened modernity. The only appropriate response, for Dawkins, is to work for the complete eradication of this deadly 'virus'. Juergen Habermas offered an alternative view, according to which the problem of 'fundamentalism' arises as a result of contradictions in the pace and process of secularisation. Its violent expression is a reaction to discordant modernisation, and is therefore itself a purely modern phenomenon (not an ancient one, as Dawkins maintained). What is called for, therefore, is a re-examination of the effectiveness of secularisation as a process of what Habermas refers to as 'creative destruction'.

René Girard's own comments on the Twin Towers attacks can be said to contain elements of each of these interpretations, in so far as Dawkins' negative description of religion *as such* would coincide with Girard's understanding of mimetic, sacrificial religion. He is closer to Habermas in seeing the problematic relationship between the antagonists, though for Girard this is expressed in terms of a mimetic hatred expressed towards the West, and a consequent rivalrous 'doubling', such as his theory describes.

The Innsbruck Research Project has offered a number of reflections on this and related themes: four joint texts have been published together (Schwager and Niewiadomski, 2003): on the Research Project itself, on Pluralism, on 11 September and a Theology of the 'Signs of the Times', and on the Israeli–Palestinian conflict. Finally, however, the words of caution expressed by James Alison in the first chapter of *On Being Liked* should be heeded, of the very real danger of Ground Zero and the events of 11 September becoming a 'sacred space' and a 'sacred event' in all the wrong senses. When he describes the atrocity thus: 'some brothers of ours committed simple acts of suicide with significant collateral murder, meaning nothing at all' (2003, p. 3), he stresses the lack of creativity of the action, but he also soberly reminds us of what we experienced in its aftermath: a 'satanic' whirlpool of heightened emotions, a frenzied search for 'meaning', and social mobilisation towards intense and of course militaristic solidarity, which for mimetic theory can only mean one thing: the beginnings of the search for a scapegoat.

Celebrating Texts

The second avenue for mimetic theory is to not worry too much about the theoretical scaffolding, and to concentrate on reading; that is, on multiplying interpretations which are 'decodings' of victimisation texts. This should not give the impression that texts are simply 'seen through' from outside, by clever people who crack the code and then go and do something else. James Alison's insistence on 'inhabiting' the story means there is more here than a 'hermeneutic of suspicion'. I think it means seeing them as texts of celebration, because in this decoding, the innocence of the victim is proclaimed – and so is our freedom and capacity to discern that innocence. In one of his bleaker poems (recording the horrors of the Irish Civil War), W. B. Yeats declares that 'the ceremony of innocence is drowned'. There are, no doubt, for Yeats, resonances in the word 'ceremony' of pretence, of formality of appearance lacking substance. Even so, mimetic theory recalls us to that ceremony and to that innocence. Again, the structure of Paul Ricœur's 'second naiveté' suggests itself.

Primary among these texts, of course, are the Jewish and Christian scriptures. What Girard has discovered and demonstrated is that the same narrative sweep – a pattern of death and resurrection, whose fulcrum is the declaration of the victim's innocence – is to be found in other texts, above all those of the great novelists and of Shakespeare. Girard has called this 'hermeneutics with a backbone'. In fact, we are confined in our reading neither to sacred Scripture nor to great fiction. Here we find an almost hallucinatory effect, as texts which are quite clearly literary and fictional coalesce with others taken from actuality. In Chapter 3, for example, a particularly gruesome short story from Kafka's *In the Penal Colony* was presented as a parable of the sacrificial machinery losing its credibility. Such an odd story surely belongs to the more bizarre and unfathomable crevices of Kafka's disturbed imagination – until we come across the intriguing account of a visit of Captain James Cook to Tahiti in 1777.

The incident is narrated in Bailie's *Violence Unveiled* (pp. 67ff), where Bailie even draws a parallel between Cook's arrival on the island and the advent of the naval officer at the end of *Lord of the Flies*! The islanders are preparing for war; a man is to be sacrificed in order to win divine favour, and Cook is invited to witness the ceremony. His status as an onlooker matches *exactly* that of the explorer in Kafka's parable, and indeed his reactions, first of rigorous questioning, then of disgust, are very similar. The parallels go even deeper. Cook finds himself outraged, not simply by the fact of the sacrifice, but also by the slipshod way in which it is carried out. If there had been a sense of sacred awe, of anything approaching a reverential attitude about the ritual, this might have redeemed it even slightly. But these are completely absent. In fact, the victim had already been killed, in secret, by the time the formal sacrificial ritual began. What strikes Cook is that the islanders no longer believe in the sacrifice they perform so half-heartedly – and therefore, like the 'Harrow' in Kafka's story, its sacral, unifying effects are negligible, and the practice itself is doomed to extinction. Cook's unbelieving presence and rational questioning have a corrosive effect, but on a ritual practice that is already losing credibility and power.

If this all looks too 'bookish', it should hardly need stressing that 'text' here refers to any cultural product that presents itself for interpretation. Mimetic theory has turned its attention to the way film and other popular media are soaked with mimetic themes. One could mention, for example, three important films which concern themselves with the death penalty. In *Twelve Angry Men* (1957), a jury has to come to terms with their illiberalism, and even racism, in order to deliberate their verdict on a murder case: a Hispanic youth from the ghetto stands accused of stabbing his father to death. Eventually, thanks to the urgings of the hero, played by Henry Fonda, the group arrives at a 'not guilty' verdict. 'No one is sacrificed' – unanimity is achieved, not by any 'miraculous' mimetic contagion, but by one man insisting upon the validity of his doubts, upon rational argumentation, and upon the presupposition of innocence until guilt has been proved beyond all reasonable doubt. The mimetic pull towards an unjust guilty verdict is, with difficulty, resisted. Coming a few years after the McCarthyite anti-communist witch-hunts in 1950s America, the film is making a very brave point indeed.

Or, two more recent film examples, more aligned with the Kafka parable we examined earlier: Robbins' *Dead Man Walking* and Kieslowski's *A Short Film about Killing* (1987) each graphically depict the state execution of a young murderer, in the United States and Poland respectively. There are, to be sure, still elements of the 'sacred victim' about the rapist and murderer, played by Sean Penn, who is executed in *Dead Man Walking* (as Edmund Arens makes clear in his essay upon this film: Arens, 1998). In the second film, however, the harrowing and lengthy hanging scene (which lasts five minutes) is so brutally pointless that it is shown to be plainly equivalent to the murder (seven minutes in duration) for which it is intended as a punishment. Its impact upon public opinion was in fact instrumental in having the death penalty taken off the statute book in Poland; *Dead Man Walking* has yet to have a corresponding effect in the USA.

It is this 'corrosive' quality that interests René Girard when he reads texts of persecution. There are two such cases of victimhood which he considers at length, separated by 600 years. The first case, which structures his argument in *The Scapegoat*, is a 'decoding' of *The Judgement of the King of Navarre*, a fourteenth-century poem by Guillarme de Machaut, which contains disguised but unmistakable references to a persecution of Jews during a time of plague. The Jews are being blamed for the epidemic, and though acts of violence against them are never explicitly mentioned, it is possible to read between the lines and understand that these did occur. Any modern reader will be clear in their own mind what has happened, and will be convinced that the Jews are innocent of the charges made against them – just as we have no doubt whatever that medieval women accused of witchcraft are innocent, even though every written record declares otherwise.

Girard wants us to pause and recognise what a startling break-through this is. We are supremely confident that we are right and the authors are wrong. Yet this breaks a basic rule of literary criticism: never do violence to the text. On this Girard is adamant: 'Faced with Guillaume de Machaut the choice is clear: one must either do vio-lence to the text or let the text forever do violence to the victims' (Girard, 1986, p. 8). The same is true of medieval records of witch-trials, where our scepticism may be even more audacious: it may be that even the accused thinks she is a witch, she may actually have tried to work harmful spells – yet still we don't believe her!

> During the trial not a single voice is raised to re-establish or, rather, to establish the truth. No one is capable of doing so. This means that not only the judges and the wit-nesses but also the accused are not in agreement with our interpretation of their own texts. This unanimity fails to influence us. The authors of these documents were there and we were not. We have access to no information that did not come from them. And yet, several centuries later, one single historian or even the first person to read the text feels he has the right to dispute the sentence pro-nounced on the witches. Guillaume de Machaut is reinterpreted in the same extreme way, the same audacity is exercised in overthrowing the text, the same intellec-tual operation is in effect with the same certainty, the same type of reasoning (Girard, 1986, p. 10).

This intellectual audacity, our confident freedom to read in this way, gives us cause to celebrate, even when reading the grimmest of persecution texts. Girard also turns his attention to the infamous Dreyfus affair which tore apart French public opinion at the begin-ning of the twentieth century (an affair, incidentally, which features in Proust's fiction). From the historical facts, Captain Dreyfus is clearly being held as a scapegoat; and yet the denunciations against him were nearly unanimous. The case for his defence is left to a few public individuals, Emile Zola being the most prominent. Finally, the truth emerges, thanks to the persistence, over years, of the pro-Dreyfus faction. In his interview with Williams, Girard declares: 'To me the Oedipus myth is a still undeciphered Dreyfus case.' Once again, the question which fascinates him is: how, by what subterranean pressure, does the truth struggle to light in situations like these?

Conclusion

In the Introduction to this book, the theme of sacral violence was introduced by a quotation from Shaw's *Saint Joan*, in which de Stogumber describes to Cauchon how witnessing the death of Joan brought home to him the reality of suffering, in a way that a lifetime of meditating upon depictions of the suffering of Christ had utterly failed to do. The event was devastating, but it had 'redeemed' him. Cauchon impatiently (or sorrowfully? or is he deeply shocked by the thought?) responds: 'Must then a Christ perish in torment in every age to save those that have no imagination?'

The mimetic theory of René Girard makes it clear that there is no easy and straightforward answer to this question. Overcoming mimetic compulsions, and turning our backs on configurations of sacred violence, may sometimes seem like a superhuman task, but conversion of the sort that de Stogumber undergoes *is* possible. What delayed the conversion in his case, and made it all the more traumatic, was his failure to connect depicted violence with the 'real' thing – his lack of imagination, as Cauchon puts it. One of the central tenets of mimetic theory is precisely a liberating dissolution of the distinction between fiction and reality. Not that reality becomes dissolved in the fictional, but that through literature and myth we are able to break through and have access to what is real ... and be redeemed.

I have suggested that these are stories by which *faith, hope and love may be challenged, confirmed, nourished, or even called into being*. Perhaps this formulation is too pompous or pious, or both. Certainly, most people will read these same medieval poems, examine the same historical texts – as well as watch the same films and flick across the same news channels – without in any way feeling a 'religious conversion' coming on. In a sense it does not matter, if we learn how to pause with occasional wonder at *what has happened* to these narratives, or more exactly, what has happened to us and the way we read them. These narratives have been turned inside out, so that they, and even our own histories of fascinated entanglement, are also stories of our liberated vision, which we can therefore inhabit with gratitude. To what, or to whom – may this not sometimes be reverently left unsaid, and when voiced, then spoken gently?

For here, perhaps, is another difference between the 'theoreticians' and the 'anti-theoreticians' among the proponents of the mimetic model. On the one hand, there are indeed projects to be formulated, 'archaeologies' to be carried out, and even battle-lines to be drawn and defended (Blake's 'mental fight'). Those committed to the mimetic model find themselves struggling for oxygen in a Western intellectual and academic climate still dominated by the 'cultured despisers', who only know how to distort, patronise or scapegoat the Jewish and Christian traditions. In spite of all that we have seen and learned, there is still a need for someone to fight Christianity's corner. And to put it mildly, René Girard himself has never backed off from these skirmishes, nor has he made any attempt to hide or excuse his political incorrectness.

On the other hand, there is a passivity, perhaps a kind of 'negative capability', which is also characteristic of mimetic theory. This means a readiness to settle into and inhabit the certainty of being forgiven or, in James Alison's phrase, 'the joy of being wrong'. It means to accept as our own a story or a drama, whose scarcely believable *dénouement* is evoked in Karl Barth's haunting words: 'the prisoner has become the watchman'. We inherit a story, given to us as miraculously and unexpectedly as Leontes receives the gift of his wife, and of himself, at the end of *The Winter's Tale*. It is a story of grace – steady, powerful and lucid, and so wondrous, apparently, that Shakespeare dared not speak its name.

René Girard, too, for all the tenacious vigour with which he has put forward and defended his theory, knows about this passivity and this joyful acceptance. This is a scholar who, when questioned about how his theory of mimetic conflict should be empirically tested, will smile and talk about watching his grandchildren at play. At the close of *Things Hidden*, he quotes at length from Ezekiel 37, seeing in the prophet's valley of death the place where present-day thought catalogues dry bones. But it is also the place where meaning, lost or threatened on all sides, simply awaits the breath of the Spirit in order to be reborn:

I hold that truth is not an empty word, or a mere 'effect' as people say nowadays. I hold that everything capable of diverting us from madness and death, from now on, is inextricably linked with this truth. But I do not know how to speak about these matters. I can only approach texts and institutions, and relating them to one another seems to me to throw light in every direction. I am not embarrassed to admit that an ethical and religious dimension exists for me, but it is the result of my thinking rather than an external preoccupation that determined my research. I have always believed that if I managed to communicate what some of my reading meant to me, the conclusions I was forced to reach would force themselves on other people as well. I began to breathe more freely when I discovered that literary and ethnological critiques are inadequate – even if they are not totally worthless – when confronted with the literary and cultural texts they claim to dominate. This was before I came to the Judaeo-Christian scriptures. I never even imagined that those texts were there for the purpose of passive enjoyment, in the same way as we look at a beautiful landscape. I always cherished the hope that meaning and life were one.

(*Things Hidden*, p. 447)

BIBLIOGRAPHY

Much of Girard's writing consists of contributions to collective works, and of articles or interviews in journals. This bibliography records all of Girard's books, and only those articles or interviews which are referred to in this work; the secondary bibliography is also a selective one.

Fuller bibliographies can be found in *The Girard Reader* (ed. James Williams; up to May 1996), and in Wolfgang Palaver's 2003 German introduction to *Girard and Mimetic Theory*.

A complete bibliography of literature on the Mimetic Theory, edited by Dietmar Regensburger, can be found under 'Girard – Dokumentation', at http://theol.uibk.ac.at/mimdok/

Girard has also contributed regularly to *Contagion: Journal of Violence, Mimesis and Culture*, which is the journal of the *Colloquium on Violence and Religion*. The proceedings of the annual Colloquium are normally published in *Contagion*; COV&R also produces a bi-annual Bulletin. Information about COV&R can be found at http://theol.uibk.ac.at/cover/

There are also contributions by Girard in some of the secondary literature, mainly addresses at conferences, *Festshriften*, etc. See particularly Adams (1993), Assmann (1991), Juergensmeyer (1992), Juilland (1985), Niewiadomski and Palaver (1995), and Swartley (2000).

The home page for the Innsbruck Research Project: 'Religion – Violence – Communication – World Order' is http://theol.uibk.ac.at/rgkw/

The home page for *Anthropoetics: The Electronic Journal of Generative Anthropology* is http://www.humnet.ucla.edu/humnet/anthropoetics/

Volume II, number 1 (June 1996) is a special issue on Girard and contains an interview with him by Markus Müller.

Works by René Girard

1962

Proust: A Collection of Critical Essays, Prentice-Hall, NY (reprinted

Greenwood Press, Westport, Ct, 1977). Edited, with Introduction by René Girard.

1965

Deceit, Desire and the Novel: Self and Other in Literary Structure, Johns Hopkins UP, Baltimore (*Mensonge romantique et vérité romanesque,* Grasset, Paris, 1961) A systematic comparison of the literary works of Cervantes, Flaubert, Stendhal, Proust and Dostoevsky, and their discovery, against the 'Romantic Lie' of human autonomy, that people form their desires according to the desires of others. This discovery amounts to a 'death and resurrection' experience for the novelists under consideration, and provides the template for Girard's subsequent development of mimetic theory.

1976

Critique dans un souterrain, L'age d'homme, Lausanne This collection of literary essays consolidates his work on Dostoevsky, with further essays on Albert Camus, Dante, Victor Hugo, Deleuze and Guattari. Some of these essays are included in the 1978 English collection.

1977

Violence and the Sacred, Johns Hopkins UP, Baltimore; Athlone, London (*La Violence et le sacré,* Grasset, Paris, 1972) In this key work, Girard traces the operation of 'the sacred' in primitive societies, thus setting out his theory of the origins of religion and culture in violent scapegoating. Crucial to his discussion are examples from classical Greek tragedy, notably Sophocles (*King Oedipus*) and Euripides (*The Bacchae*); the book also includes important chapters on Sigmund Freud and Claude Lévi-Strauss.

1978

'To double business bound': Essays on Literature, Mimesis and Anthropology, Johns Hopkins UP, Baltimore; Athlone, London Essays, including some from the earlier French collection (1976). In addition, Girard writes here on Nietzsche, Richard Wagner and Lévi-Strauss, once again. The volume includes an interview with Girard which first appeared in *Diacritics* 8 (1978).

1986

The Scapegoat. Johns Hopkins UP, Baltimore; Athlone, London (*Le Bouc émissaire,* Grasset, Paris, 1982) Girard considers a historical text – a medieval poem – to illustrate how we look for indications of persecution in our reading, and seeks to extend this way of reading to mythological texts, offering a set of criteria for 'the scapegoat'. He considers some myths in detail (e.g. Teotihuacan), and a number of chapters are devoted to mimetic readings of gospel passages (the Passion narratives, The Demons of Gerasa, the role of the Holy Spirit in history).

1987a
Things Hidden Since the Foundation of the World, research undertaken in collaboration with Jean-Michel Oughourlian and Guy Lefort, University Press, Stanford Ca. (*Des Choses cachées depuis la fondation du monde*, Grasset, Paris, 1978)
Girard's most extensive work, though not the most accessible. It takes the form of a three-way, and fairly technical, conversation between Girard and two psychiatrists. The first third of the book, entitled 'Fundamental Anthropology', assesses the plausibility of the scapegoat theory in the light of current thinking in ethnology and other human sciences; the second part examines sacrifice in the Judaeo-Christian scriptures, setting up the contrast between the 'logos' of Heraclitus and the *Logos* of John. The final third of *Things Hidden* is concerned with 'Interdividual Psychology', in which the notion of mimetic desire is expanded into a theory of sexuality, and in which Girard's differences with Freudian theory are made explicit.

1987b
Job: the Victim of his People, Athlone, London (*La Route Antique des hommes pervers; Essais sur Job*, Grasset, Paris, 1985)
A short collection of readings of the book of Job as a persecutory text.

1987c
'Generative Scapegoating' in Hamerton-Kelly (ed.) 1987, *Violent Origins*, pp. 73–105
This colloquium brings Girard's mimetic theory into focus alongside that of Walter Burkert's *Homo Necans*, and the work of Jonathan Z. Smith. These different approaches are scrutinised in turn, as their respective authors attempt to find common ground. Burton Mack's introductory assessment of mimetic theory, and Girard's own essay, are very useful.

1988
'The Founding Murder in the Philosophy of Nietzsche' in Dumouchel, P. (ed.) *Violence and Truth*, Athlone Press, London, pp. 227–246
Girard concludes the colloquium with a mimetic reading of Nietzsche's affirmation in *The Gay Science* of the 'death of God'.

1991

A Theatre of Envy: William Shakespeare, Oxford University Press (reprinted Gracewing Press, England, 2000)
A series of essays on Shakepeare's drama, as illustrated by mimetic desire, which includes close readings of *A Midsummer Night's Dream, Julius Caesar* and *A Winter's Tale*, as well as of James Joyce's speculations about Shakespeare in *Ulysses*.

1993

'A Conversation with René Girard' in Adams, R. (ed.), 1993
This essay is important for Girard's recognition that he had changed his views on sacrifice since *Things Hidden,* where he admits to having 'scapegoated' the letter to the Hebrews and the notion of Christian sacrifice.

1994

Quand ces choses commenceront . . . Entretiens avec Michel Treguer, arléa, Paris (*Wenn al das beginnt . . . ein Gesprach mit Michel Treguer*, Lit Verlag, Munster, 1997)
An important in-depth interview with Girard, not translated into English, which contains an overview of the mimetic theory, the fullest account to date of Girard's religious conversion, as well as discussion of key topics such as democracy and contemporary politics, freedom, Freud and structuralism.

1996

The Girard Reader, ed. James Williams, including 'The Anthropology of the Cross; a Conversation with René Girard', pp. 262–88
An invaluable resource for coming to terms with mimetic theory. Selections from Girard's writings are used to provide an overview of the theory, as well as its three different 'parts'. There is a section on Girard's relationship to Freud and Nietzsche, while the *Reader* also includes an interview with René Girard, a glossary, and a bibliography of works in English, French and German.

1997

Resurrection from the Underground: Feodor Dostoevsky, Crossroad, New York (*Dostoievski: Du double a l'unité*, Plon, Paris, 1963)
Girard's second book, though not translated for over thirty years, explores the theme of mimetic desire in Dostoevsky's fiction, with particular emphasis on themes such as the 'Doppelganger', *ressentiment* and triangular desire in e.g. *The Eternal Husband.*

2001a

I See Satan Fall like Lightning, Maryknoll, New York (*Je vois Satan tomber comme l'éclair*, Grasset, Paris, 1999)
This short book continues Girard's exposition of the biblical revelation as the means by which mimetic scapegoating is challenged and overcome. It begins with an interpretation of the Decalogue as a set of prohibitions on mimetic desire.

2001b

Celui par qui le scandale arrive, Desclée de Brouwer, Paris
Not translated into English. Under the title *Contre le relativisme* are three essays, two of which have appeared elsewhere: on violence and reciprocity, on cultural relativism, and on mimetic theory's relevance for theology. There is also an extensive interview with Maria Stella Barberi, entitled 'L'envers du mythe', which considers many aspects of the biblical revelation, historical and contemporary Christianity, Lévi-Strauss, deconstruction, and other topics.

2004

Les Origines de la Culture, Desclée de Brouwer, Paris
An overview and re-examination of the anthropology of mimetic theory in response to questions from Pierpaulo Antonello and Joao Cezar de Castro Rocha.

Works concerning René Girard

Adams R. (ed.), special edition of *Religion and Literature* 25.2, Notre Dame Indiana, 1993, includes, 'A Conversation with René Girard: Interview by Rebecca Adams'

Alison J., *Raising Abel: The Recovery of the Eschatological Imagination*, Crossroad, NY, 1996

Alison J., *The Joy of Being Wrong: Original Sin through Easter Eyes*, Crossroad, NY, 1998

Alison J., *Faith beyond Resentment: Fragments Catholic and Gay*, DLT, London, 2001

Alison, J., *On Being Liked*, DLT, London, 2003

Anon., *To Honor René Girard*, Stanford French and Italian Studies, Anma Libri, Ca., 1986. Presented on the occasion of his sixtieth birthday by colleagues, students, friends. With full bibliography pp. iii–xxxii, including references to interviews and reviews in French.

Arens, E., 'Dead Man Walking', *Contagion*, vol. 5, Spring 1998

Assmann, H. (ed.), *Sobre idolos y sacrifios: René Girard con teologos de la liberacion*, Coleccion Economia-teologia, San José, Costa Rica: Editorial Departmento Ecumenico de Investigacones, Petrópolis, 1991 (*Götzenbilder und Opfer: René Girard im Gespräch mit der Befreiungstheologie*, Lit Verlag, Thaur, 1996)

Auden, W. H., *Collected Poems*, Faber and Faber, London, 1976

Bailie, G., *Violence Unveiled: Humanity at the Crossroads*, Crossroad, NY, 1995

Balthasar, Hans Urs von, 'Die neue Theorie von Jesus als dem "Sündenbock" ', *Communio* 9, 1980, pp. 184–5.

Balthasar, Hans Urs von, *Theo-Drama: Theological Dramatic Theory* IV: 'The Action', Ignatius Press, San Francisco, 1994 (Theodramatik: Dritte Band 'Die Handlung', Johannes Verlag, Einsiedeln, 1980)

Bandera, C., *The Sacred Game: The Role of the Sacred in the Genesis of Modern Literature*, Pennsylvania State University Press, University Park, 1994

Barstow, A. L., *Witchcraze: A New History of the European Witch-Hunt*, Pandora/HarperCollins, NY, 1995

Burkert, W., *Homo Necans: the Anthropology of Ancient Greek Sacrificial Ritual and Myth*, Berkeley, Ca., 1983 (1972)

Chilton, B., *The Temple of Jesus: His Sacrificial Program Within a Cultural History of Sacrifice*, University Park, Pennsylvania, 1992

Chilton, B., 'Sacrificial Mimesis', *Religion* 27, 1997, pp. 225–30

Daly, R., *The Origins of the Christian Doctrine of Sacrifice*, Fortress Press, Philadelphia, 1978

Daly, R., 'Sacrifice' in Fink, P. (ed.), *New Dictionary of Sacramental Worship*, Gill and Macmillan, Dublin, 1990, pp. 1135–37

Daly, R., 'Is Christianity Sacrificial or Anti-sacrificial?', *Religion* 27, 1997, pp. 231–43

Daly, R., 'Violence and Institution in Christianity', *Contagion*, Spring 2003, pp. 4–33

Davis, C., 'Sacrifice and Violence: New Perspectives in the Theory of Religion from René Girard', *New Blackfriars* 70, 1989, pp. 311–28

Domenach, J.-M., 'Voyage to the End of the Sciences of Man', in Dumouchel P. (ed.), 1988, pp. 152–59

Duff, P., 'The Sacrificial Character of Earliest Christianity: A Response to Robert J. Daly's "Is Christianity Sacrificial or Anti-sacrificial?" ', *Religion* 27, 1997, pp. 245–48

Dumouchel, P. (ed.), *Violence and Truth: on the work of René Girard*, Athlone, London, 1988 (*Violence et vérité: autour de René Girard*, Grasset, Paris, 1985)

Eagleton, T., *The Illusions of Postmodernism*. Blackwell, Oxford, 1996

Eagleton, T., *After Theory*, Allen Lane, London, 2003

Flaubert, G., *Madame Bovary*, Everyman Edition, London, 1993

Fleming, C., *René Girard: Violence and Mimesis*. Key Contemporary Thinkers, Polity Press, 2004

Gans, E., *The Origin of Language: A Formal Theory of Representation*, University of California Press, 1981

Gans, E., *The End of Culture: Toward a Generative Anthropology*, University of California Press, 1985

Gans, E., *Science and Faith: The Anthropology of Revelation*, Savage, Md.: Rowman & Littlefield, 1990

Gans, E., *Originary Thinking: Elements of Generative Anthropology*, Stanford University Press, 1993

Gans, E., Introduction in *Anthropoetics: The Electronic Journal of Generative Anthropology*, volume II, number 1, June 1996: http://www.humnet.ucla.edu/humnet/anthropoetics/

Galvin, J. P., 'Jesus as Scapegoat? *Violence and the Sacred* in the Theology of Raymund Schwager', *The Thomist* 46, 1982, pp. 173–94

Galvin, J. P., 'The Marvellous Exchange: Raymund Schwager's Interpretation of the History of Soteriology', *The Thomist*, 1989, pp. 675–91

Gauchet, M., *The Disenchantment of the World: A Political History of Religion*, Princeton, 1997

Golsan, R. J. (ed.), *René Girard and Myth: An Introduction*, Garland Publishing Inc., New York and London, 1993. Theorists of Myth 7, with bibliography pp. 181–237.

Goodhart, S., ' "I am Joseph": René Girard and the Prophetic Law' in Dumouchel (ed.) 1988, pp. 53–74

Goodhart, S., *Sacrificing Commentary*, Johns Hopkins UP, Baltimore, 1996

Hamerton-Kelly, R. (ed.), *Violent Origins: Walter Burkert, René Girard, and Jonathan Z. Smith on Ritual Killing and Cultural Formation*, Stanford University Press, Stanford, 1987

Hamerton-Kelly, R., *Sacred Violence: Paul's Hermeneutic of the Cross*, Fortress Press, Minneapolis, 1992

Hamerton-Kelly, R., *The Gospel and the Sacred; The Politics of Violence in Mark*, foreword by René Girard, Fortress Press, Minneapolis, 1994

Hobbes, T, *Leviathan*, edited by Richard Tuck, CUP, Cambridge, 1991 (1651)

Irigaray, L., 'Les femmes, le sacré, l'argent', *Critique* 42, 1986, pp. 372–83

Jay, N., *Through your Generations Forever: Sacrifice, Religion and Paternity*, University Press, Chicago, 1992

Juergensmeyer, M. *Violence and the Sacred in the Modern World*, Frank Cass & Co, London, 1992

Juergensmeyer, M. (ed.), *Terror in the Mind of God*, University of California Press, 2000

Juilland, A., (ed.), *To Honor René Girard: Presented on the occasion of his sixtieth birthday by colleagues, students and friends*, Stanford French and Italian Studies 34, Anma Libri, Palo Alto, Ca., 1985

Kafka, F., *The Complete Short Stories*, Vintage, London, 1999

Kojève, A., *Lectures on Hegel's Phenomenology of Spirit*, Basic Books, 1969 (1934)

Kofman, S., 'The Narcissistic Woman: Freud and Girard', in Moi, T. (ed.), *French Feminist Thought; a Reader*, 1987 (1980), pp. 210-26

Lacey, A. R., *A Dictionary of Philosophy*, Routledge and Kegan Paul, London, 1976

Loughlin, G., 'René Girard: Introduction' in Ward, G. (ed), *The Postmodern God, a Theological Reader*, Blackwell, Oxford, 1997, pp. 96-103

Lorenz, K., *On Aggression*, Bantam Books, New York, 1967

McKenna, A. J., 'René Girard and Biblical Studies', *Semeia* 33, 1985, Introduction, pp. 1-11

McKenna, A. J., *Violence and Difference: Girard, Derrida and Deconstruction*, University of Illinois Press, Urbana and Chicago, 1992

Mack, B, 'The Innocent Transgressor: Jesus in Early Christian Myth and History', *Semeia* 33, 1985, pp. 135-65

Mack, B, 'Introduction: Religion and Ritual' in *Violent Origins*, ed. R. Hamerton-Kelly, 1987, pp. 1-73

Milbank, J., *Theology and Social Theory: Beyond Secular Reason*, Blackwell, Oxford, 1990

Milbank, J., 'Stories of Sacrifice', *Modern Theology* 12, 1996, pp. 27-56

Moi, T., 'The Missing Mother: the Oedipal Rivalries of René Girard', *Diacritics* 12, 1982, pp. 21-31

Moltmann, J., 'Covenant or Leviathan? Political Theology for Modern Times', *Scottish Journal of Theology* 47, 1994

Niewiadomski, J. and Palaver, W. (eds.), *Dramatische Erlösungslehre: Ein Symposion*, Innsbrucker Theologische Studien 38, Tyrolia, Innsbruck, 1992

Niewiadomski, J. and Palaver, W. (eds.), *Vom Fluch und Segen der Sündenböcke: Raymund Schwager zum 60. Geburtstag*, Kulturverlag, Thaur, 1995

Niewiadomski, J. and Wandinger, N. (eds.), *Dramatische Theologie im Gesprach: zum 65. Geburtstag von Raymund Schwager*, Lit Verlag, Munster, 2003

Nietzsche, F., *On the Genealogy of Morals*, Oxford World Classics, OUP, 1996

Nowak, Susan, 'The Girardian Theory and Feminism: Critique and Appropriation', *Contagion*, Spring 1994, pp. 19-29

Oughourlian, J. M., *The Puppet of Desire*, Stanford University Press, California, 1991 (*Un Mime Nommé Desir*, Grasset, Paris, 1982)

Palaver, W., 'A Girardian Reading of Schmitt's Political Theology', *Telos* 93, 1992, pp. 43-68

Palaver, W., 'Hobbes and the Katéchon: the Secularization of Sacrificial Christianity', *Contagion* 2, Spring 1995, pp. 37-54

Palaver, W., *René Girards mimetische Theorie*, Lit Verlag, Munster, 2003

Proust, M., *In Search of Lost Time*: vol. 1, Vintage, London, 2002

Reineke, M., ' "The devils are come down upon us": Myth, History and the Witch as Scapegoat' in *The Pleasure of her Text: Feminist Readings of Biblical and Historical Texts,* ed. Bach, A., Trinity Press, Philadelphia, 1990, pp. 117–45

Ricœur, P., *Freud and Philosophy,* Yale University Press, New Haven, 1970

Rike, J., 'The Cycle of Violence and Feminist Constructions of Selfhood', *Contagion* 3, Spring 1996, pp. 21–42

Schwager, R., *Must There be Scapegoats? Violence and Redemption in the Bible,* Harper & Row, San Francisco, 1987 (*Brauchen wir ein Sündenbock? Gewalt und Erlösung in den biblischen Schriften,* Kosel, München, 1978)

Schwager, R., 'Christ's death and the prophetic critique of sacrifice' in McKenna (ed.), 1985, pp. 109–123

Schwager, R., *Der Wunderbare Tausch: Zur Geschichte und Deutung der Erlösungslehre,* Kosel, München, 1986

Schwager, R., 'The Theology of the Wrath of God', in Dumouchel, P. (ed.), 1988, pp. 44–52

Schwager, R., *Jesus and the Drama of Salvation,* Crossroads NY, 1992 (*Jesus im Heilsdrama: Entwurf einer biblischen Erlösungslehre,* Tyrolia, Innsbruck, 1990)

Schwager, R., & Niewiadomski, J., *Religion erzeugt Gewalt: Einspruch!* Lit Verlag, Munster, 2003

Scheler, M., *Ressentiment,* Marquette Studies in Philosophy, 2003 (1915)

Schweiker, W., 'Sacrifice, Interpretation and the Sacred: the Importance of Gadamer and Girard for Religious Studies', *Journal of American Academy of Religion* 55/4, 1989, pp. 788–810

Schweiker, W., *Mimetic Reflections: A Study in Hermeneutics, Theology, and Ethics,* Fordham UP, New York, 1990

Scubla, L., 'The Christianity of René Girard and the Nature of Religion', in Dumouchel, P. (ed.), 1988, pp. 160–78

Shakespeare, W., *Complete Poems and Plays,* Oxford UP, 1965

Swartley, W. M. (ed.), *Violence Renounced: René Girard, Biblical Studies and Peacemaking,* Telford, 2000

Vawter, B., *On Genesis; a New Reading,* Chapman, London, 1977

Wallace, M, and Smith, T. (eds), *Curing Violence,* Polebridge Press, Sonoma, Ca., 1994

Webb, E., *The Self Between: From Freud to the New Social Psychology of France,* University of Washington Press, Seattle, 1993

Williams, J., *The Bible, Violence and the Sacred: Liberation from the Myth of Sanctioned Violence,* HarperCollins, San Francisco, 1991

Williams, J. (ed.), *The Girard Reader,* Crossroad, NY, 1996, including interview with René Girard, pp. 263–88

Wink, W., *Engaging the Powers,* Fortress Press, Minneapolis, 1992

INDEX

CPSIA information can be obtained at www.ICGtesting.com
Printed in the USA
BVOW032306250112

281404BV00005B/1/P